This book is dedicated to

My mother, who was the inspiration for the English Courtyard Association

and Phyllis, without whose love, encouragement and support

I would have achieved precisely nothing!

December 2012

Front Cover Photograph: *St. Luke's Court, Marlborough*

Noel Shuttleworth and Christopher Thornhill, and their architects the Siddell, Gibson Partnership, revolutionized the idea of retirement in the early 1970s, setting new standards of building and management and providing a truly English solution for those wishing to enjoy an elegant, independent and secure lifestyle from early retirement onwards.

This is an inspiring story describing the events that led up to that achievement, and the people involved. It also furnishes a very useful guide for those who are considering retirement and wanting the best, as well as those who wish to make the best possible provision for their future needs.

It is a personal account of the background to, and history of, the English Courtyard Association, its successes, its failures and its unfinished business, all of which offer ideas and information that others may wish to take further.

Foreword

The inspiration for the English Courtyard Association, and the events leading to its formation, grew from the needs of my widowed mother and of those from the professional and landed classes. Born towards the end of the reign of Queen Victoria, my mother's generation lived and served through two horrendous world wars and the depression of the 1930s. They put duty to their country first, and made the huge sacrifices from which their children and grandchildren benefit today. They were entitled to comfort and security in retirement, and it became the aim of the English Courtyard Association to attempt to provide it.

This book gives me the opportunity to thank all those that brought about the creation of the Association, as well as sharing thoughts and ideas for others to consider.

In particular my thanks are due to:

Christopher Thornhill, co-founder of the English Courtyard Association, without whom this book could never have been written. I also acknowledge with gratitude the major contribution he made to many of the original ECA drafts and documents used in this book.

Paul Gibson and his fellow architects Giles Downes CVO and Richard Morton of the Sidell Gibson Partnership, who between them designed all 37 of our Courtyard developments.

Paul Greenwood, whose support in the early days was invaluable.

All those Courtyard Managers who were prepared to go the extra mile to provide our residents with the happy, secure environment and quality of life to which they are entitled, and all those ECA residents, past and present, who have supported and encouraged us so loyally over the past 35 years.

Peter Hussey, Courtyard Manager of St. Luke's Court, for his technical advice and encouragement, and for arranging for this book to be published.

Carol Geddes, former editor of Courtyard Views, for her general assistance and advice, and for permission to use several articles and photographs previously published in Courtyard Views.

Richard Morton, partner in Siddell Gibson & Partners, for architectural advice and assistance.

My thanks are also due to:

Former ECA Board Members Bruce Sharman, Brigadier Michael Owen, Angela Barker and Stephen Alexander FCA, for their advice and support.

Gay Gardner, banker, adviser and lifetime friend.

John Galvin and The Elderly Accommodation Counsel: www.eac.org.uk

Peter Burden OBE, writer, journalist and ECA resident, for advice and introductions.

Colin Philp, principal photographer, responsible for most of the photographs in the chapter on 'The Courtyards'. colinphilp@hotmail.com

David Zeke, photographer, for photographs of Froxfield, The Wardrobe and Motcombe Grange.

Common Ground, for kind permission to use their photograph of apple trees. www.commonground.org.uk

Wikipedia, for background information on Courtyard locations.

Although I am the author of this book, and the views expressed in it are mine, any credit for ECA's success is shared equally with my partner and friend Christopher Thornhill.

Contents

Chapter I

The Beginning

The English Courtyard Association was my brainchild. Born in Leeds, the son of a Church of England clergyman, I was educated at Haileybury College and the Royal Military Academy Sandhurst. Following my commission in the Scots Guards, I served in Germany, Canada, Kenya and London. On leaving the army with the rank of major, I began a career in marketing with Courtaulds. I subsequently went into business producing a special gold coin issue for the Kenya Government in conjunction with Spink and Sons, and then moved into the fashion industry before joining a major public relations and marketing consultancy in 1968. Three years later, on Friday 13 August 1971, I suffered a serious car accident which left me in a wheelchair and quite severely disabled for some 18 months. This experience was not only to prove of great advantage in my future career, but was a defining moment in my life. For during this period of enforced leisure, my widowed mother was facing problems in trying to find a suitable home to be near her son. As a result I returned to active life in 1973 determined to find a workable solution.

In my childhood, the families of most professional people had staff, and elderly relations were largely cared for at home. Therefore, as the son of a country parson, brought up in the large rambling rectories of North Yorkshire, it was quite natural to me that first my grandmother, and later a great-aunt, should live there too.

But after the war things started to change; fewer people had domestic staff, so other solutions had to be found. Many independent elderly people retired in style, taking suites of rooms in the luxury hotels of Bath, Cheltenham, Harrogate and other spa towns, or by the sea. But by the end of the 1950s, many of these hotels had decided to concentrate on the conference trade. This resulted in their sumptuous spacious bedrooms, with their ornate bathrooms, being subdivided into two – or even four – box-like rooms with showers, to meet the demands of this new market. Permanent residents were no longer welcome; indeed, they were actively discouraged.

During this same period, local councils and newly-formed housing associations were starting to build flats for the elderly to rent. There were of course nursing homes, and some 'granny flats' were built, either by caring families and relations, or sometimes by young families looking for a live-in babysitter on the cheap!

Almshouses, built and endowed by wealthy local landowners, benefactors and philanthropists, had existed for the poor and elderly of their parishes since the 12th century. By the 1970s they had largely come under the umbrella of the Almshouse Association. Many of them, like those at Froxfield (between Marlborough and Hungerford) were magnificent Tudor and Elizabethan buildings, but many were in need of modernization and repair.

The practice of the poor and elderly being looked after by their parishes had dramatically changed with the Agricultural Revolution, when many able-bodied farm workers were put out of work and made destitute by the introduction of modern farm machinery. Then in 1834 the Poor Law was introduced, and with it the creation of 5,000 workhouses within ten years, which transferred responsibility for the poor and elderly from the villages to the government, where it has largely remained.

By the beginning of the 1970s, it was recognized for the first time that there was a need to provide proper housing not only for the poor and elderly, but for a whole new market – the elderly of the professional classes.

An opportunity arose for me to do something about it when a neighbour, Major General Thuillier, asked me to assist with – and to join the committee of – the Savernake Housing Association, which he and his wife Barbara had formed, in order to provide accommodation and assistance for local retired professional people. Clements Meadows, the former home of the world famous jockey Sir Gordon Richards, had been acquired in Marlborough. A local architect had drawn up plans for its conversion, and planning permission had been obtained. However, by early 1973 it was already becoming apparent that insufficient charitable funding would be forthcoming to finance the venture.

If the Clements Meadows project were to proceed it needed a change of direction, so I agreed to set up a rescue plan. Although the Committee did not like or endorse the plan, or the use of commercial monies for what they believed to be a purely charitable enterprise, they recognized that substantial debts had already accrued to the charity and that my method was probably their only realistic hope of recovering these debts. In December, General Thuillier finally agreed that I should be given the opportunity to put my plan into action.

In conjunction with Paul Greenwood of John D Wood, and committee member Malcolm Young, formerly chairman of Ross Foods, a plan was drawn up and agreed. Instead of the proposed rented bedsitting-rooms, one-bedroom apartments would be developed for sale on a 70-year lease, with a service charge to cover maintenance, heating, lighting, furnishing and cleaning of the common parts, and the provision of two main meals a day. Such a scheme would be unique in the area and it was felt that there would be considerable demand for it.

The first thing was to verify the demand. Two small advertisements, in the personal columns of the *Times* and the *Daily Telegraph*, offering these services to owner occupiers, produced over 120 replies, clearly confirming the potential demand for such a scheme.

John Divett, a friend and former property adviser to the Bankers Trust, now himself a successful property developer, was impressed, and willing not only to become involved but to underwrite the scheme. He introduced me to a young architect, Paul Gibson of the Sidell Gibson Partnership (at that time a newly- formed architectural partnership based in London, and today one of the leading architectural practices in the UK), which he ran with his partner Ron Sidell. Ron was in the process of completing the second of two major office blocks in Frankfurt for John Divett and his commercial partner, property giant MEPC. I became Paul's first client!

Paul Gibson redesigned Clements Meadows, with one wing consisting of 40 new purpose-built one-bedroom apartments for sale, at the end of which was a solarium. On the ground floor, the main house contained a large main hall and office, two reception rooms, two dining rooms, kitchen, laundry, sluice and storage. The communal rooms led out on to a terrace and an attractive garden.
Upstairs were two self-contained staff flats, each with an adjoining sitting room,

LOWER LEVEL PLAN 1:20(
OLD PEOPLES HOUSING
CLEMENTS MEADOW MARLBOROUGH
SIDELL GIBSON PARTNERSHIP ARCHITECTS
3 ALBION STREET LONDON W2 262 5462
DRAWING 25/12 APRIL 1974

whilst the first floor of the wing, accessed by a passenger lift and staircase, contained a medical staff room, treatment room, shower and four private wards, leading on to a veranda overlooking the garden. Outside, at the rear of the buildings, was a pleasant garden and summer house, whilst at the front of the main house there were some 20 parking places.

My mother, in those days, was a typical customer of Barclays Bank Trust Company. A widow with a share portfolio of some £80,000, she was – like thousands of other such people – neither rich nor poor. Barclays Bank Trust Company managed her financial affairs.

I therefore decided to approach D.G. Hanson, the General Manager and Director of Barclays Bank Trust Company, with a view to the Trust Company both financing the development and acting as Trustees. Mr Hanson liked the idea and agreed to look into it further. However, he thought it would be more interesting to the Trust Company if sales of the properties were conducted in shares rather than cash.

In view of the Trust Company's positive interest, it was felt that Divett, Young and Shuttleworth should form a company, bound by a service contract with Barclays Bank Trust Company, to carry out the following tasks:

> To find suitable sites for the building of retirement homes for the elderly;
> To negotiate the purchase of the agreed sites;
> To plan and build the required facilities;
> To organize the marketing of the facilities in conjunction with the local offices of Barclays Trust Company;
> To organize, with the local offices of Barclays Trust Company, the setting up of Trust Funds;
> To arrange, together with the local offices of the Trust Company, the purchase and sale of shares in the Trust Funds; and
> To organize and oversee the running of the retirement homes by:
> - setting up registered charities to administer the non-profit making day-to-day running of each home, and
> - supplying qualified management to run the home for each charity.

Barclays Bank would supply the necessary finance, at the request of Barclays Trust Company, to purchase agreed sites, build and market the homes.

On completion of the building and sale of all the properties, the freehold of each development would be transferred to a Trust Fund, which would be administered by the local branch of Barclays Trust Company.

*****

It all looked extremely promising, but finally the Trust Company and Barclays Bank balked at funding the operation unless the financial risk was underwritten elsewhere, although the Trust Company remained interested in acting as Trustees.

However, by now the economic climate was so grim that John Divett was no longer prepared to underwrite the scheme either, and approaches to friends at Hambros and Flemings and other financial institutions ended with the same result.

By the early 70s there were three main charities providing assistance for the elderly: Help the Aged, the National Corporation for the Care of Old People, and Age Concern. Help the Aged and the National Corporation for the Care of Old People had both formed housing associations – the Anchor and Hanover Housing Associations. Both organizations built for rent, with funding coming from the government, via the Housing Corporation. Age Concern had a wide network of offices, but no building arm.

There was one last chance...

Approaches were made to Hanover Housing Association through Colonel Hackett, Director of the Almshouse Association, who was also Vice President of Hanover Housing Association. He appeared seriously interested and a revised plan was made.

The Revised Plan for Clement Meadows

Barclays Bank Trust Company agreed to participate in the setting-up of a national network of retirement homes for middle income purchasers. The first of its kind was to be Clements Meadows in Marlborough.

The Trust Company authorised its branch office in Reading to set up the Barclays Savernake Trust Fund, in which the residents of Clements Meadows retirement home would be required to purchase shares, the sales price of the shares to be 1/40th of the full cost of the development. Payment of these shares was to be made by each resident prior to their taking up occupation.

The National Corporation for the Care of Old People, through the Hanover Housing Association, was to be responsible for the construction and running of the retirement homes. (Hanover was already a nationwide organization, with a total of 3,200 flats either completed or under construction, in over 30 counties of the United Kingdom. Hanover was also interested in extending its operations to include the largely-neglected middle income market.)

Planning permission, in outline form, had been granted by Kennett District Council for Clements Meadows, and we already had the names of 80 people who were interested in becoming residents.

Barclays Bank, at the request of the Trust Company, had intimated its willingness to put up 100% of the finance for the construction, on the understanding that repayment + interest would be guaranteed by a fixed date, approximately twelve months after the completion of construction.

Barclays Bank Trust Company would assist with the marketing by passing on information via their local offices to those of their clients who might be interested in Clements Meadows and the services it offered.

The structure still left room for the Clements Meadows Fundraising Committee to raise additional money to assist the financially less well off. (The fund originally had previously received promises of £125,000 in donations.)

*****

The Plan, as envisaged, provided an excellent blueprint for future retirement developments. It brought together 'blue chip' companies expert in their respective fields. It combined the trusteeship of Barclays Bank Trust Company, finance provided by Barclays Bank, construction and management by a leading national charity for the elderly, and the opportunity to raise further charitable funds to help the less well off. All that remained was to obtain a guarantee to underwrite the scheme from the Housing Corporation.

The Housing Corporation, effectively a government housing bank, provided virtually 100% of the finance for the Hanover and Anchor schemes. As Hanover were to carry out the construction and the management of Clements Meadows, it seemed a 'racing certainty' that the Housing Corporation would agree to the guarantee. But, as with many such racing certainties, this was not to be the case. The Housing Corporation refused to give the guarantee, and the plan collapsed.

So, in the spring of 1975, Clements Meadows was sold. It was a bad day for everyone involved. The Housing Corporation normally fully financed Anchor and Hanover schemes for rent, which meant that they had huge sums of money tied up in these buildings for long periods. But in this case, all the Housing Corporation was being asked to do was to provide a guarantee. Since all properties at Clements Meadows were to be sold, it was extremely unlikely that it would have cost the Housing Corporation anything – certainly infinitely less than the cost of building any development for rent.

Furthermore, if sales were to be conducted in shares as opposed to property, it allowed the guarantor additional safeguards. For example, if there were 40 flats and the actual total cost of the building was £400,000, in order to fully recover the cost each flat would need to be sold for £10,000. The purchaser would purchase and receive certificates for 10,000 one pound shares in the fund set up by Barclays Bank Trust Company.

However, if sales were slow and it became necessary to reduce the price of a flat to, for example, £9,000, then the share system would allow for 'shared ownership'. The purchaser would receive 9,000 one pound shares, whilst the guarantor would retain 1,000 shares in the property.

Each year, or on resale, Barclays Bank Trust Company would revalue the shares to take account of fluctuations in their value – up or down – in the property market. On resale of the property, vendors would receive the current market value of their 10,000 one pound shares, while on the resale of a property in shared ownership the vendor would receive payment for 9,000 shares and the guarantor would receive payment for 1,000 shares at their current market value.

In addition, since the scheme was 'not for profit' and the properties were being sold at cost, there would be no developers' profit to be paid. This could mean savings of 20-30%, as the developers' risk factor would have been removed from the equation by the Housing Corporation guarantee.

An added benefit was that the Housing Corporation could have used its position to control and regulate fair and affordable prices for future resales, at Clements Meadows and at all such schemes built in future, to a figure no greater than the original value of the property, plus the annual rate of inflation (as opposed to house inflation). This would have been fair to the owners, as it would have ensured that the value of their property was protected, whilst restricting them from profiteering on their sale, a mechanism that would have ensured that properties remained affordable for future purchasers.

Thus a huge opportunity to provide a national pool of housing for elderly owner occupiers, at both controlled prices and minimal government risk, was lost.

But this opportunity almost certainly could still exist today, or in the future. Perhaps such an experiment could be tried in conjunction with the Prince's Trust?

*****

Although it was now too late for Clements Meadows, the seed for the future had been sown. There was clearly a market for the Clements Meadows idea, but almost certainly one funded not by charitable but by private finance. The answers to the advertisements in the *Times* and *Daily Telegraph* had clearly shown that many people wanted and needed this type of accommodation, and were prepared to pay for it themselves. They did not need charity, just the right accommodation, good management and a fair deal.

I refused to be despondent. In conjunction with Paul Greenwood of John D Wood, who provided me with office space at his office in Newbury, and architect Paul Gibson of the Sidell Gibson Partnership, I was determined to pursue the goal.

Chapter II

The Worcestershire Hotel at Droitwich

The Worcestershire Hotel

From my childhood, I remembered the grand hotels of Harrogate, and this gave me the idea. They offered the opportunity of a 'Clements Meadows' on a grand scale.

By the 1960s and 1970s the pre-war lifestyle of the 1950s had changed dramatically. The hotel industry was changing too, and a large number of hotels were on the market at this time. This was due in part to their change from residential to conference trade use and in part to the increase in motorway construction, which changed people's habits, enabling many to travel out and back in a day rather than stay overnight in a hotel. This particularly affected the country house and market town hotels, many of which, by the early 1970s, were closing down and being sold. Many of them were quite cheap to buy, as they were largely being valued on falling turnover rather than on their property value which was usually much higher.

In Marlborough, in 1971, there were two large hotels: the Marlborough Arms and the Castle and Ball. Following the construction of the M4, however, the town was effectively bypassed and today only the latter remains, the former having been turned into an office block. This was typical of what was happening nationwide.

Robert Barry & Co. and Christies, in particular, specialized in hotel sales, so with their assistance the chase was on to find a suitable grand hotel that could be divided into sumptuous apartment suites for sale, whilst continuing to offer those in retirement all the facilities of a luxury hotel. The most suitable were likely to be found by the seaside or in spa towns. For although life was changing, many still hankered for the more graceful lifestyle and service that they had known before the war.

After a number of false starts I discovered the Worcestershire Hotel at Droitwich. This seemed to meet all the requirements.

Droitwich, a small spa town of some 20,000 people, five miles from Worcester, just over 20 miles from Birmingham, and five miles from two junctions with the M5, had been built on sandstone and rock salt, and had been famous since Roman times for its production and distribution of salt, and its brine wells and springs.

In the early nineteenth century a cholera epidemic gave rise to the 'discovery' that bathing in its briny waters apparently produced a miraculous cure, and its fame as a spa town was born.

In 1891 John Corbett, the 'Salt King', built the Worcestershire Brine Baths Hotel, later to be renamed the Worcestershire Hotel. In its heyday it was described as 'the finest in Britain'.

In 1974, the hotel was owned by Donald Robinson, a Scotsman who also owned the Bramley Grange Hotel at Bramley in Surrey. Both hotels were on the market, and I investigated their possibilities. (By coincidence, some 28 years later, following a devastating fire, the Bramley Grange Hotel was sold and the site bought for the Beechcroft Trust by Guy Mossop and Henry Thornton. Today it is managed by Cognatum Ltd., which was formed in 2010 when the management of all English Courtyard Association and Beechcroft Trust properties was merged.)

Of the two, the Worcestershire Hotel seemed to meet the requirements perfectly. Built in the last years of Queen Victoria, the hotel still embodied the feeling of opulence and prosperity associated with its past, through the comfort of its luxuriously furnished common rooms, its excellent cuisine and its service.

The hotel contained 100 bedrooms, 70 with en-suite bathrooms, family suites, private dining suites, conference rooms, bridge rooms, cocktail bar, banqueting suites, facilities for private dinner parties and dinner dances – indeed, formal dinner dances were held in the hotel most Saturday nights. There was parking for 100 cars and some lock-up garages, and an 18-hole miniature pitch-and-putt golf course.

The hotel lent itself easily to conversion. Paul Gibson swiftly drew up designs for 57 flats, each consisting of a single or double bedroom, a sitting room, bathroom and kitchenette, and facilities for television and private telephone.

Communal areas for residents' use included four drawing rooms, a restaurant/dining room, private dining rooms, a bar and a card room, five bedrooms for residents' guests, ladies' and gentlemen's cloakrooms, and three launderettes.

Services provided included lunch and dinner in the dining room, lunch and dinner for guests (with 24 hours' notice), morning coffee and tea for residents and guests, bar service, cleaning of common parts, central heating throughout the building, fuel and electricity, repairs and maintenance, and garden maintenance

It is important to emphasize that all services were to be on a non-profit making basis, therefore catering for residents and their guests could be done at cost. Since the management was able to buy in bulk, food and drink could be produced more cheaply than if privately or individually purchased.

Staff costs included:

Resident Manager and an assistant (one of whom would be always on the premises)

Lunch and dinner seven days per week

Rates

Fuel, electricity and heating

Laundry (communal)

Cleaning of communal areas

Repairs and maintenance to communal and external areas

Management of garden

Management fee to caterers

Obviously, since our residents were by definition elderly, some consideration had to be given to long-term nursing care. It was accepted that nursing requirements would need to be reviewed by a charitable board and/or a residents' committee, which would need to be formed. Nursing requirements for residents would be examined within the theme and framework of 'total security', although it was recognized that the Worcestershire was not a nursing home, nor was it intended that it should become one.

*****

The first thing required was to bring in expert management to run the hotel services. Sutcliffe Catering, who had wide national experience, agreed to undertake the catering contract, and Michael Matthews, formerly Chairman of Trust Houses Group (before they merged with Forte Holdings, eventually to become Trusthouse Forte), offered to come on the Board and oversee the running of the hotel services.

Running costs for the hotel, submitted by Sutcliffe Caterers and approved by Michael Matthews, when divided equally by 50-plus apartments, were extremely reasonable, whilst meals, including a proper lunch and dinner served in the dining room, were costed at just over £1 per person per day!

Barclays Bank Trust Company was still prepared to act as Trustees, and Paul Greenwood and John D Wood agreed to take charge of marketing. Strong interest was being shown by Help the Aged's subsidiary, Guardian Housing Association, with a view to their acting as managing agents, and an impressive list of potential Board Members, selected locally, had been approached and agreed to serve on the Board. Day-to-day management would be carried out by the managing agents, with input from a residents' committee.

Guardian, who had recently commenced construction on a development for owner-occupiers at nearby Bromsgrove, also wished to involve John D Wood in the sale of their own properties. These were currently undergoing difficulties and Guardian was interested in joining forces if private money could be found to purchase the hotel. But it was not within the Housing Corporation's remit to fund such a grand scheme, even with Guardian's participation.

Once again the hunt was on for finance. But by the late summer of 1975, it looked as if the problem had been resolved. Christopher Thornhill, a friend and contact of Paul Greenwood, had expressed serious interest.

Christopher had been an estate agent in the early 1970s before switching to property development, and indeed still had a small estate agency, Stanbrook and Thornhill, in north London. During the past few years he had specialized with some success in the conversion of London flats, using his own firm Euclid Conversions, and employing a small group of builders. The company was named after a horse that won the Derby in the nineteenth century, with which Christopher's family had some connection. (From 1981 - 2000, Noel and Christopher used Stanbrook and Thornhill to handle all the ECA resales).

In late 1974 Christopher had bought the Draycott House Hotel in Chelsea, a small private hotel on the corner of Draycott Avenue and Draycott Place, with the intention of converting the hotel into flats for sale, but the market turned against him. A friend of Christopher's was George Steer, a former banker who had become Chairman of Chasophie Ltd., a subsidiary of the Bonas Group; following a suggestion by Christopher's former partner Peter Seddon, and with George Steer's assistance, the Bonas Group bought the hotel and turned it into luxury serviced apartments on short-term lets, with the intention of appealing particularly to the American tourist trade. Draycott House filled a gap in the market; its success was assured from the outset and later cemented when Jane Renton, who had previously held a senior management position at the Dorchester Hotel, became the General Manager. Jane was a brilliant choice and between them she, George and Christopher turned Draycott House, over the next 20 years, into the best-known luxury service apartment hotel in London. Their clientele were genuine celebrities from all walks of life – when the word 'celebrity' actually meant something!

The Bonas Group, a family firm based in Hatton Garden, were the largest rough diamond brokers in the world. Benjamin Bonas had inherited the firm from his father, and George Steer was his right hand man. One of George's main roles was to expand the Group's interests into other fields, using Chasophie Ltd. as its vehicle, so that the firm would become less dependent on the diamond trade. The Bonas Group was one of a select few diamond brokers that brokered on behalf of de Beers, but in the 1970s the future of South Africa and the diamond trade could certainly not be taken for granted. Despite the strength of the South African economy, apartheid had brought with it a false sense of security.

Although Christopher Thornhill liked the idea of the Worcestershire Hotel he would not be rushed, even though by now time was becoming important. Understandably, he refused to finalize any agreements until Draycott House was up and running to his and the Bonas Group's satisfaction. As a result, there followed a longish period of enforced delay. But by mid-1976 Christopher was ready and willing to commit resources, and appointed John Argent of Philip Pank & Partners as Quantity Surveyor and the late Nick Goodwin as his Surveyor.

By now, everyone was confident that the purchase of the Worcestershire Hotel would finally take place. An 'off the shelf' Friendly Society, September Properties, had been acquired by lawyers Linklaters and Paines to undertake its ownership and management and Paul Greenwood was able to write to them, on 3 July 1976: '*a decision has been made to go ahead with this scheme and a visit will be made to Droitwich… at which an undertaking will be made to the vendor that contracts will be exchanged within three weeks or possibly less from that meeting, obviously assuming that no disasters are uncovered by the surveyors*'.

But by the end of the month everything had changed. The surveyor's report was deemed unacceptable. There was probably more to it than just that. Undoubtedly there was some apprehension amongst those responsible for financing the venture that the scheme involved heavy management overheads, but, whatever the reasons, the result was the same. The purchase of the Worcestershire Hotel would not proceed.

Chapter III

Collaboration with Christopher

The decision not to proceed with the Worcestershire Hotel came as a great shock, and was hugely disappointing to those closely involved. It also coincided with the decision to withdraw the hotel from the market. Michael Matthews, the former chairman of Trust Houses, wrote that as a result of the delay in reaching a decision we had not only *'missed the bottom of the market but also missed premises that would be as near to ideal for this purpose as one is likely to find in an imperfect world'*.

But it was not all doom and gloom. George Steer had accepted that there were *'many attractive features to this or a similar scheme'*, although *'not in its present financial form'*. He had also noted that *'we have the skills to do this job better than anyone else – it is our sort of work and our scale of project and I am confident from the work that has been done that there is a strong market for the product at this sort of price level.'*

Christopher Thornhill was also enthusiastic but strongly of the opinion that if we were to bring such a scheme to a successful conclusion, and expected the house owning public to invest their money in property (instead of just care), then it had to be in a form of ownership that they understood, i.e. freehold or long leasehold. Moreover, he firmly believed that the private sector would be suspicious of being sold anything unusual along with a property, since insurance and financial services had not worked for estate agents. He felt that adding care, food, etc., and confusing such extras with property ownership, would in 1976 be equally unacceptable. It was agreed not to proceed on this basis.

A decision was taken, therefore, for Christopher and me to collaborate, and on 1 August 1976 I became a consultant to Geometer Developments, based at 8 Holland Street, Kensington, originally on a three-month contract, whilst we worked out exactly what we wanted to do and how we were going to do it. It became my base for the next 25 years and the beginning of a hugely innovative and successful partnership that set the standards of construction and management of quality retirement housing for all time.

If I was the originator of the idea, turning the idea into reality could not have been achieved without the brilliance – indeed, genius – of my partner Christopher Thornhill. Christopher was born in 1940, the son of a former naval captain and a Maltese mother who was a serious musician. From her came his skills on the piano and his beloved 'squeeze box'. He was never happier than when playing at his own parties, surrounded by family, friends and colleagues. But his first love undoubtedly was the sea, and his sailing boat *Sai See*, in which he and his wife Valentine and their two children Katharine and Mary travelled the length and breadth of the British Isles, and much further afield besides. Later they would sail with some regularity to Guernsey, where the English Courtyard Association established Les Blancs Bois, their only Courtyard development outside the UK.

In due course, Christopher became Commodore of the Royal Cruising Club of Great Britain, which he administered from what was almost his second home – the Royal Thames Yacht Club. Christopher was educated at King's School, Bruton, from which he was known at times to run away – even at a young age needing to escape the cloistered life of a boarding school! Friends suggest that it was not until his days at King's College, Cambridge, and the scholastic challenges and opportunities that Cambridge offered, as well as its freedom, that he came into his own. And he liked obscure challenges. Even his degree at Cambridge was in Medieval French and German! He learnt and retained information amazingly quickly, and had a quick and enquiring mind. When confronting a problem, he had the ability to get to the nub of it, dissect it, remove what was inappropriate and present it in a logical light. He never had architectural training, but even in his days as an estate agent his real interest was in building and conversion. With his brilliant and practical mind, he learnt 'on the job', and could interpret architects' drawings and see in his mind exactly what the finished article would look like. This skill allowed him to modify the design – the proportions, or the amount of space between buildings – and the detail, such as the selection of the appropriate brick or tile. Indeed, he had taught himself all the skills of a really great architect. His brilliant brain also allowed him to write, concisely and clearly, drafts for brochures, pamphlets, reports.

Most importantly, Christopher was a perfectionist; he wished to achieve excellence, and the creation and implementation of each development had to be as near perfect as possible. Once a site had been bought, he would never attempt to skimp or save money if it involved lowering the English Courtyard standard. He was driven, not by profit but by the desire to achieve excellence, a factor that sometimes caused irritation amongst those responsible for financing our developments, to whom he was always extremely loyal. Certainly the English Courtyard Association – and our residents that have lived at our developments – should always be grateful to him for his sense of priorities!

******

In 1976, apart from Guardian Housing Association, there were virtually no organizations that provided private retirement housing for sale, other than the Country House Association and Retirement Lease Housing Association. Of these, only the Country House Association offered accommodation suitable for those both used to and requiring a high standard of living, but none of CHA's developments were new build; they were all conversions of grand houses.

The Country House Association (originally formed in 1955 as Mutual Households) had, as its primary aim, the preservation of historic buildings for the nation. By the early 1970s the Association had acquired nine large country houses, some with freehold, others on long fully repairing leases, all of which had been restored and converted into retirement apartments with communal dining and drawing rooms. There was a rental charge intended to cover the service charge, and the extensive renovation and repair of the houses as well as the maintenance of their large grounds. The residents paid for their apartments with loan stock, which at that time was depreciated by 3% per annum. If a resident became elderly and needed nursing they were required to move into a nursing home. The Association eventually went into liquidation at the end of 2003.

Retirement Lease Housing Association was founded by two formidable ladies, Margaret Webb and Louisa Hawken, to whom I had been introduced by Valerie Green, the then Secretary of the National Federation of Housing Associations. RLHA had completed its first development in 1973 and had several others in the pipe-line. They offered fairly basic modern flats and bungalows for sale on lifetime leases, but the owners or their heirs only received back their original investment when the property was resold.

Much was learned – about what to do and what not to do – from these two organizations. But another major factor, that was becoming ever more important, was that by 1976 inflation was running close to 20% per annum! This meant that capital protection had to become an important plank in Christopher's and my philosophy – something that no other provider of private retirement housing seemed to have taken into account. It had become essential for retired people investing in a retirement property to have their capital protected as far as possible, so as to provide funds both for nursing homes if and when they became necessary, and for that very English middle-class basic requirement – to leave as much money as possible to their children and grand-children.

There were other factors. Although grounds were very important, living down long drives and being cut off from village life was probably not ideal. The thought, too, that at any Country House Association development you could be forced into a nursing home because there was no opportunity for you to have living-in help was also a matter of concern, as was the huge cost of maintaining large Grade 1 & 2 listed buildings.

Slowly ideas began to formulate.
*****

The first requirement was to find a suitable site. Christopher and I required a site of between three and five acres within easy flat walking distance of good basic shopping, near the centre of an attractive market town or large village. Ideally the site should possess a medium-sized house of some architectural merit – so as to set the architectural tone – but not too large, as new build would provide the best opportunity to create individual views, as well as the right size and type of accommodation.

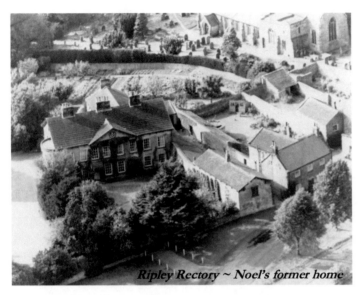
Ripley Rectory ~ Noel's former home

Hotel sites were still a possibility, and having been reared in large rural rectories in North Yorkshire I was only too aware of the excellent opportunities these sites offered. However, by now the Church too had become aware of their development potential, the size of their grounds being more than sufficient to allow the construction of a small new vicarage or rectory, whilst offering the original for sale as a private house.

Farms also were sited in the centre of expanding villages, but the picturesque sight of herds of cows and flocks of sheep blocking country lanes no longer suited a 'modern' society! So many village farmyards were moving further afield, and their farmhouses and farmyards were being sold. Other sources of information included the Historic Buildings Bureau and of course local estate agents, though the latter proved less useful than one might have presupposed, due – perhaps understandably – to estate agents being more interested in being retained for the sale of the new houses that would be built on the land than in the sale of the land itself, something that neither Christopher nor I were in a position to guarantee.

Many sites were viewed over the next two months. Two of these were to prove both exciting and influential, and were responsible for creating the 'courtyard' idea that was to become the trademark of all the English Courtyard Association's developments.

Information about the availability of The Wardrobe in Salisbury Close came from an unexpected source: the quarterly report of the Department of the Environment's Historic Building Bureau. This 150-page tome describes *'buildings statutorily listed as being of historic or architectural interest for which the Historic Buildings Bureau are anxious to assist the owner to find a user'*. Originally the home of one of the canons of the Cathedral in the sixteenth century, it had since undergone many alterations and changes of use over the ensuing years. But, in the shade of Salisbury Cathedral, one of the most perfect settings in England, The Wardrobe clearly offered great opportunities, not only for the conversion of the house itself into a number of magnificent apartments, but because it offered the opportunity to build a number of new houses in its grounds leading down to the river.

Close to my home in Wiltshire was the Duchess of Somerset's Hospital at Froxfield, a magnificent development of Tudor almshouses, one third of which were dedicated for the occupation of widows of the clergy. Thirty cottages surrounded a tranquil rectangular courtyard in the middle of which stood a Gothic chapel, rebuilt in 1813 by her descendant, the then Earl of Ailesbury. It did not take great imagination to realise that the cottage scale and design of Froxfield would be perfect for the new houses at The Wardrobe.

The Wardrobe, Cathedral Close, Salisbury

Paul Gibson approved the site and provided plans and sketches. I first submitted these informally to the Dean of Salisbury, Fenton Morley, who by chance had been a friend of my mother for many years and whose support would be essential if this scheme were to be brought to fruition. The Dean liked the idea in principle.

Christopher and I visited Froxfield together and met a number of the residents of the almshouses. We both had some concern about building a development on two floors for the elderly, and all the almshouse cottages were on two floors. But this concern was totally allayed when one elderly resident of many years' standing, on being asked if she was worried by the stairs in her cottage, replied that she would 'go

18

upstairs to bed every night if it takes the last breath in my body to do so!' So – on her advice – the cottage idea came to fruition.

Another significant site was Barton End in the attractive market town of Alton in Hampshire, which had recently come on the market. Barton End was an ideal site of some 2½ acres including a pleasant Georgian house, probably the former Rectory, which until recently had been the offices of East Hampshire District Council, which had moved to new offices at Penns Place, Petersfield.

Alton was a perfect town for our first scheme – a country market town, well equipped with shops and with fast rail connections to London. Barton End was ideally situated, just off the High Street and close to the Church of St. Lawrence. Unlike The Wardrobe, it was unlikely to present planning problems, and indeed early discussions with the planning authorities confirmed that there would be little difficulty in our obtaining suitable planning permission. Christopher and I were agreed that Alton was the right place!

But firstly there was a need to resolve how our developments were to be managed. Twenty-five properties were too few for us to consider setting up our own management structure, and the minimum required to make the service costs affordable, so an alternative had to be found. Discussions took place with the local branch of Age Concern, but they felt that the housing we were proposing was too expensive and luxurious and did not fit in with their image.

I had previously been in touch with Louisa Hawken at Retirement Lease Housing Association and set up a meeting with her for Christopher and myself at their Farnham offices, which resulted in RLHA agreeing to become managing agents for the Barton End project. We were now ready to submit our proposals to the planning authorities.

Proposed Accommodation for elderly people at Barton End

"The aim of the development is to provide retirement accommodation for the middle income group – the section of society that Councils do not have the financial resources to assist. On completion the scheme will be managed by Retirement Lease Housing Association that has wide experience in this field.

A number of flats and small houses will be grouped around the central building and the pleasant garden setting will be maintained.

The central building is an attractive Georgian house, deep eaved, with a slated roof. The surrounding new buildings will be designed to harmonize with this style, so that the effect of development will be 'traditional' and it will avoid the appearance of a very modern building.

The dwellings will be specially designed for elderly people and will incorporate the following features: -

Kitchen and bathroom will be non-slip.
Bathroom fittings will be selected for elderly people.
Doors and lifts will be wide enough for wheel chairs.
Special attention will be given to details such as window and door catches.
Ample storage will be a feature of all types of dwelling.
There will be an easily activated alarm system with bells and indicator boards at strategic points throughout the complex.
All buildings will be centrally heated.
Television points will be provided.

Residents will be entirely independent and will be able to lead their own lives without unwelcome interference from anyone. There will be a resident secretary/warden who will be on call in case of need or emergency and whose duty will be to see to the general administration of the scheme and help residents with any problems that arise.

Residents will purchase their own dwellings in the usual way and there will be an annual charge to cover the cost of the secretary, garden, general maintenance etc.

The scheme will consist of a mixture of flats and cottages.

The flats will be on the ground floor, first floor and upper floors only and there will be a lift to the upper floors. There will be one and two bedroom flats.

The cottages will be in small rows, two-storied, built round the edge of the gardens. They will be designed in versions, with one or two bedrooms upstairs, and will be adaptable so that a person who becomes infirm can live entirely on the ground floor, without the need to go upstairs.

Running Costs and Service Charge

It is envisaged that residents will be responsible for their own normal household expenses such as:-

Rates
Insurance
Gas
Electricity
Telephone etc.

An annual charge will be made to cover:

The general maintenance of the buildings
The upkeep of the grounds and gardens

The secretaries/wardens
The general administration costs
The cost of communal facilities (i.e. Laundry Room)

The services will be provided at <u>cost</u>: there will be no element of profit for the management.   The annual cost will be divided between the residents, who will be able to see the full accounts.

Tenure

The dwellings will be sold on long leases (at least 60 years).

A resident will be the owner of the dwelling and will be able to sell it on the open market, subject to the provision of the lease.

The lease will be similar to an ordinary long lease of a house or flat, but there will be special clauses concerning: -

The provision of the services. Particularly the secretary/warden and the communal facilities.

Restriction on the age of the residents to ensure the character of the scheme, as retired accommodation for retired people, is maintained.

A clause stating when, in the opinion of a suitably qualified committee, a resident can no longer manage his/her own affairs, he/she may be required to leave Barton End, subject to reasonable notice.

The sale of Barton End was to be by tender, and on 24 June 1977 we submitted our tender. However, Christopher remained unhappy about two things. We were aware that it was possible that the owner of an adjoining property benefited from a covenant, dating from 1817, precluding building on the site we wished to purchase *'that would intercept the view in front of the dwelling houses on the North side of Lenten Street.'* The other factor was that, although the District Council had clearly indicated that our proposal had been accepted, they had not actually given us planning permission, nor were they prepared to do so until we owned the site.

Our tender for Barton End was the highest, but we were still anxious to resolve our outstanding concerns, and submitted them to the Council. But the Council made no offer to help resolve them and instead offered the site to the under-bidder, who accepted it with alacrity and – adding insult to injury – later used our plans to build a similar but much inferior development.

Then, to rub further salt into our wounds, we learned that The Wardrobe in the Cathedral Close at Salisbury had been offered to the Wiltshire Regiment as their regimental museum as it was felt – understandably – that they had a better claim to it than we had. We were devastated. It seemed that the culmination of years of work was about to fall apart.

But fate was on our side. That weekend, on my way out to dinner, I saw a For Sale sign at Manor Farm, Pewsey. Next day I investigated the site and talked to Paul Bowerman, the owner, whom I knew socially. Paul intended to sell the farmyard site but for the time being to retain the Manor. It seemed too good to be true, and an opportunity that we could not afford to miss. The farmyard site offered everything that Barton End had to offer. Pewsey even had a fast train service to London. There was no time to be lost. As Christopher was not available, I rang George Steer, who had a weekend house very close to me at Wootton Rivers. Together we visited the site. We both realised that this could be the answer to our prayers – and our last chance. Immediately, George put things in train to purchase the farmyard.

However, there was still the question of obtaining planning permission. Applications for five and six houses had been turned down, and to make a viable scheme we needed twenty-five! Paul Gibson, our architect, went with me to see the Chief Planning Officer, Mr Payne, who was extremely helpful. Having looked at the plans for Barton End he confirmed that he liked the scheme and would like to see something similar at Manor Farm. He advised us that if we were prepared to put in a planning application with a Section 52 agreement, which limited the occupiers of the properties to being over the age of 55, it would receive his support.

By the end of November 1977, Manor Court had been acquired!

Chapter IV

The English Courtyard Association

Four years' research had evolved into what was to become the English Courtyard concept. Christopher and I were agreed on three things: who it was for, what we wanted to achieve, and how we would achieve it.

The 'courtyard' idea sprang from memories of our school and university days. The beautiful courtyards of Oxford and Cambridge, particularly at Trinity College, had been an inspiration to Christopher, whilst I drew mine from the magnificent Quad at Haileybury, which had originally been built in 1810 as the training college for the East India Company.

The other major architectural influence was the Duchess of Somerset's beautiful Elizabethan almshouses at Froxfield, between Marlborough and Hungerford. The idea, the architecture and the setting – the church, the manor, the stream, the cricket field, the village shop – were all quintessentially English.

Almshouses at Froxfield

Almshouses at Froxfield

The buildings were to be built for, and based on, the needs of 'our own' – our parents and relations. The buildings needed therefore to be traditional, offering style and sufficiently spacious accommodation to enable their residents to retire with dignity, in comfort and security.

They were designed, unashamedly, for what used to be called the 'professional classes' and 'country landowners'. Retired officers from the army, navy and air force; the church; the colonial and civil services; former bankers, accountants and captains of industry; doctors, professors, teachers and senior nursing staff – such people were the backbone of England. Also to be considered were those who still identified with the English countryside, who perhaps had handed over their large country houses and estates to the next generation, and now wanted to retire to live a quiet country life, but one in which they could still contribute albeit in a more modest way

During the past 30 years many examples of all the above have found a happy and rewarding life – and friends – at English Courtyard Association developments.

It is worth remembering that, at this time, neither McCarthy and Stone nor the words 'sheltered housing' were in existence. The English Courtyard Association was breaking entirely new ground, and in its first ten years both it and its architects were showered with serious architectural, landscape and housing design awards. The Association was in direct competition with entries from every category of building, not just those in the retirement field, but it was recognised and rewarded as a force for innovation by the Royal Institute of British Architects, the Department of the Environment, the National House Building Council and the Civic Trust.

Meanwhile the following decisions had been taken. Paul Gibson and his assistant Giles Downes were appointed architects for Manor Court. Retirement Lease Housing Association was to be responsible for overseeing day-to-day management, whilst Paul Greenwood and John D Wood were in charge of sales and marketing of the properties.

But as yet no name had been selected for the organization that would be ultimately responsible for agreeing the design and overseeing the management and the sale of the properties, and would inherit the freehold of the development from the development company once the final property had been sold.

Christopher, Paul Greenwood and I met at 8 Holland Street, off Kensington Church Street, which was to be the company offices for the next 20 years, and after some discussion it was agreed that the new organization should not be personalized, thus ideas like 'The Shuttleworth Trust' or 'The Thornhill Trust' were considered unacceptable.

Paul Greenwood was the first to come up with the name 'Courtyard', which Christopher immediately endorsed, and it was left to me to embellish it by adding 'The English' and 'Association'.

The name was agreed – subject to confirmation of acceptability at Companies House – and The English Courtyard Association was born.

Christopher and I were to be Directors, Governors and sole Members of the English Courtyard Association. Its Members legally controlled the Association and could, as necessary, appoint further Directors or remove them. I was to be its Chairman, a post I held for the next 34 years.

Christopher was already managing director of Geometer Developments, the development company which was a subsidiary of the Bonas Group. Stephen Alexander FCA, already Secretary of Geometer Developments, became the new Secretary of the Association.

The Memorandum and Articles were drawn up by Ian Lockhart of Peake and Co of Bedford Square (later Ian became Senior Partner of Charles Russell but remained the Company's senior legal adviser) and the new company was registered as a non-profit making company limited by guarantee in early 1979 – six years after my first 'inspiration'!

The following facts may be of interest and are listed here for clarity:

1. The English Courtyard Association was formed as – and remains – a non-profit making company
2. All ECA developments were designed jointly with our development company, Geometer Developments Ltd, and our architects the Sidell Gibson Partnership, and sold under the ECA banner.
3. Geometer Developments – later English Courtyard Developments Ltd. – was until its sale in 2006 a subsidiary of Chasophie Ltd., the investment arm of the Bonas Group of Companies, and responsible for the financing of all ECA's developments.
4. The Bonas Group of Companies is a substantial privately-owned family business, whose principal interests are in the diamond fields.
5. Once all ECA's properties have been sold, their freeholds revert to ECA. Today ECA owns the freeholds of all their properties except those at Motcombe Grange, Dorset, where several properties still remain unsold.

Chapter V

The English Courtyard Association Management

The Courtyard Manager

The cornerstone of the management of all English Courtyard Association developments, its success and the happiness of our residents, has always been the Courtyard Managers and their willingness to go the extra mile, way beyond what should be expected of them. In the appointment of the Courtyard Managers, with only a very few hiccups, the Association has been extremely fortunate in the quality and dedication of those attracted to the position.

June and Peter Hussey Courtyard Managers St Luke's Court

The name 'Courtyard Manager' evolved with time. At Barton End their job description was 'Resident Secretary'. However, by the time Manor Court, Pewsey had been acquired it had changed to 'Warden.' There were those that thought the word institutional, whilst its defenders maintained that it was an old English word, and if it was good enough for the Queen Mother to be called Warden of the Cinque Ports and for some of our most distinguished residents to be Wardens of Oxford colleges, it should certainly have been good enough for the English Courtyard Association! Nonetheless, by the mid-90s the name was finally changed to 'Courtyard Manager', although the word 'warden' is still commonly used when describing the Courtyard Managers' 'caring' role.

Originally, in 1979, Manor Court employed one Courtyard Manager, who lived on site in a two-bedroom flat overlooking the Courtyard (the excellent Mrs Robinson, a former nurse) and also contract gardeners. But after a year, Mrs Robinson left the Association; she felt that her job was too stressful for one person to cope with without support, or a shoulder to cry on if a resident unwittingly upset her. The job required two people. Tied in with this was the fact that residents felt that the service they were receiving from the contract gardeners was unsatisfactory. They tended not to turn up if the weather was inclement, and due to their other commitments they never caught up, so the maintenance of the gardens suffered and fell below expectations.

The result was that from 1980 onwards two Courtyard Managers were employed to live on site, in accommodation provided by the Association. Usually they would be a husband and wife team, one largely undertaking the 'caring' role and the other – normally the husband – being responsible for the garden and security.

The Association has often been asked, 'What is the role of the Courtyard Manager?' First and foremost it is that of being a 'good neighbour' – advising on all the services that are available in the area and places of interest, helping those who may not be able to do for themselves such things as changing light bulbs or putting cases up into the loft, and ensuring that new residents are introduced and made to feel welcome.

But the list of duties and responsibilities stretches much further, to maintaining and testing the alarm system on a regular basis, looking after anyone who falls sick until proper help is in place and liaising with families, keeping a discreet eye on those who have become frail or lonely but without interfering in their privacy which is sacrosanct, arranging for workmen's visits to carry out maintenance for

A minibus service is available at many Courtyards

the development or for residents, helping to arrange for cleaners or carers, organizing the booking of the guest suite and the laundry on a fair basis, and – at those developments that have one – driving the minibus. In addition, Courtyard Managers liaise as necessary with Head Office staff, as well as assisting with those many technological problems that arise from a new digital age – televisions, computers, mobile phones – and a million other things with which residents may be glad of their help. Their principle aim is to provide a happy and secure environment for the enjoyment of all their Residents.

This is a personal service that the Association provides 365 days a year. If the Courtyard Managers are off duty, a Relief Manager is available. Their help in an emergency is always available 24 hours a day and is the first port of call. The knowledge of this often gives as much comfort and reassurance to the residents' families as it does to the residents themselves, and frequently obviates the need for a resident to move into a nursing home unless and until absolutely necessary.

It needs to be appreciated that at any one time younger residents may need the service less than those that are frail. Younger residents are more likely to be glad of the security that the Courtyard Managers provide. It allows them to go away, perhaps abroad, on a cruise or to visit family or friends, knowing that their property is safe and the garden being maintained in their absence. But younger residents, in time, become older and will then be equally glad of the 'caring' service that the Courtyard Managers provide.

Although their role is to oversee the running, security and maintenance of their site in the best interests of all their residents, it needs to be recognized that the Courtyard Managers are not servants, nor are they there to nurse residents on a permanent basis.

The English Courtyard Association is not just about bricks and mortar, spacious accommodation and beautiful gardens, it is also about the service and quality of life that the Association offers. The Courtyard Managers play a key role in getting this message across. Purchasers of ECA properties need to understand that they are buying the Courtyard Managers, and the service which they provide, every bit as much as they are buying the property itself. It is their service that increases the value of the property, and that service is, in part, what residents are purchasing.

Explaining exactly what the Association can offer, and what the Courtyard Managers can offer, is essential when it comes to the resale of a resident's property. From the earliest days, the Association maintained comprehensive lists of all those who visited our developments, showed interest in our properties and asked to be placed on the mailing list. But it is the Courtyard Managers who show visitors over their development, the properties that are available and the grounds, highlighting the things that are likely to be important to each. They will then ensure that visitors' names and addresses are recorded so that they are informed as and when any property, at any development in which they are potentially interested, becomes available.

Although residents or their families have always been able to sell their properties privately or through an estate agent if they wish, the great majority of all resales have come from, and benefited from, using the Association's own Resale Service, which is supported by national advertising and the huge amount of additional knowledge and information that the Courtyard Managers are able to provide. This is something that few, if any, estate agents are able to provide. They are used to valuing and selling houses, not houses and services specially built for retirement. It is always wise, therefore, for those wishing to sell an ECA property to use the ECA Resale Service first, and perhaps later – should the sale be taking longer than might be expected – to do so in conjunction with a local estate agent.

******

Senior Management

In 1979, the day-to-day management, as mentioned previously, although overseen by Christopher Thornhill and myself, was carried out by Retirement Lease Housing Association. Whilst Louisa Hawken remained at the helm this worked extremely well, but those that took over after her retirement were not in the same class. They appeared unenthusiastic in either meeting residents or dealing with their problems. However, they did have an excellent local manager, Lynne Jamieson (later Lynne Jamieson-White), who was responsible for overseeing the Association's fourth development at Lyefield Court, Emmer Green.

It was becoming clear that the Association needed to take control of its own management, and, with four completed developments and one underway at Puddletown in Dorset, it was now large enough to do so. Fortunately I was able to persuade Lynne Jamieson to become the Association's first General Manager. Based first at her home and later at offices nearby in Broadstone, Lynne did a wonderful job. She was extremely efficient, and nothing was too much trouble; she ran a very happy team and, together with the accountant and secretarial staff, built up a wonderful rapport with residents and Courtyard Managers alike, thus helping create the English Courtyard Association 'family'.

Indeed there was a strong family feel about the Association from the outset. Whenever a new development was being built, many existing residents would attend one of the regular Open Weeks, and have a glass of wine with Christopher or myself – or those holding court – to check on what the latest ECA development had to offer that they did not have! However, nearly always their parting remark would be, 'We liked it very much, but we still think ours is the best!'

The family feel was strengthened by the Chairman's chatty winter, summer and autumn News Letters to all residents and all those on the Association mailing list (later to be succeeded by the more professional and excellent – but perhaps less 'homely' – Courtyard Views, which some considered too sales-oriented) and Lynne's ability to keep close personal contact with both residents and staff.

*****

As time passed and the Association grew, the need arose for more sites and in early 1990 Christopher and I appointed Victor Kidd as site finder and land-buyer, a role previously largely carried out by myself. I had originally met Victor at Warnham in East Sussex at one of Retirement Lease Housing Association's earliest developments, when he was their development officer. He proved an excellent choice at both finding new sites and dealing with planning applications. In the fifteen years that he worked for us he never had a planning permission refused, or lost an appeal: a most impressive record of which he was quite rightly very proud. He had a very good understanding of what was required to obtain a planning consent and was deeply committed to our organization and took great pride in the fact that he worked for the English Courtyard Association. Sadly Victor died in January 2010.

The need had also arisen for – at first – part time 'local' managers, and later full-time Regional Managers. The first of the latter were Martin Osborne and Charles Clayton. Martin, in time, became Regional Manager of the Southern Region and Charles of the Northern Region.

Charles Clayton was to become a significant figure in the evolution of the English Courtyard Association. Having joined the Association on a part-time basis in September 1991, as local Manager for Framers Court, Charles took on wider responsibilities in June 1993 and on the creation of the Northern Region in 1998 became its Regional Manager - and the General Manager in 2000. In 2001 Charles was invited to join the Board and became Managing Director of the Association.

Born and brought up in Sheffield, Charles moved to London in 1970 to work for the Community Service Volunteers on various projects with disabled young adults, the elderly and the homeless. In 1972 he joined the Spastics Society (now Scope) in an administrative capacity. In 1980 Charles changed direction, becoming Estates Manager and later Head of Property Services for another organization, managing 60 residential, educational and industrial premises, in the process gaining technical building qualifications and becoming a member of the Chartered Institute of Building. Then he started his own company advising on disability access for large institutional owners. He dissolved this company when the opportunity came for him to work full-time for the English Courtyard Association.

Charles' wide and varied previous experience of national charities, of the building trade and of the elderly and disabled, as well as his excellent administrative and communication skills and friendly personality, proved invaluable in the multi-faceted requirements of his role as the Association's Managing Director. From the outset he concentrated on communication with both Courtyard Managers and Residents alike and was largely responsible for the Association's management being voted, in 2008, the best in the country for 'overall service' and 'value for money' by the Association of Retirement Housing Managers.

By 2001 the Board needed to change. Whilst I remained Chairman of the Board, I had semi-retired and was in ill health with chronic emphysema. To assist Charles Clayton, Stephen Alexander, who had left the development company, joined the Board. Stephen had been both Chief Accountant and Company Secretary to the Association – and its extremely loyal servant – since its formation, and his experience and knowledge of the Association were invaluable.

Charles advised further changes to revamp and modernize the ECA Board, the most important of which was the introduction of a Resident Director. As the title suggests, this is a director who, being a resident, can help to ensure residents interests are properly represented in the Association's decision making process. The Board welcomed this idea, and the first of these – Alan Plastow – proved the ideal choice. An Oxford and Fulbright scholar, Alan became Personnel Director of May and Baker, and later of ASDA, before going on secondment as Regional Director for Yorkshire and Humberside to Business in the Community, headed by HRH The Prince of Wales. There in just over two years he was responsible for creating almost 9000 new jobs in his Region. The success of this appointment led, following Alan's retirement in 2005, to the Board appointing two more distinguished residents as Resident Directors: Brigadier Michael Owen and Bruce Sharman. Later, when it became necessary to separate the Association from the development company and take the decision to merge the Association with the Beechcroft Trust, it was decided to increase the number of Resident Directors to four by adding Angela Barker and Sir Idris Pierce. All Resident Directors played a major role in assuring the Association's future.

There were two other significant changes to the Board. In 2005 Christopher Thornhill had a stroke, and although he was briefly to return to the ECA Board he was unable to continue as managing director of the development company.

Chasophie Ltd. replaced Christopher as Managing Director of the development company, which by this time had assumed the name English Courtyard Developments, with Tom O'Brien, an astute accountant. As it was the Board's practice to have a representative from the development company on their Board, so that both organizations could work harmoniously together, Tom also joined the Board of the English Courtyard Association.

I had been extremely concerned for some time about the lack of executive support for Charles Clayton. Neither I nor Stephen Alexander was in good health, and the worry 'What if anything should happen to Charles?' was a serious one.

But a chance meeting proved fortuitous. One evening at my club, the Cavalry and Guards Club, a member sitting at an adjoining table asked my name. He was Christopher Mackenzie-Beevor, then the Club's Vice Chairman, today its Chairman. He recognized my name immediately and told me that he was a great fan and admirer of the English Courtyard Association.

Originally Christopher had been much concerned, and had thoroughly disapproved, when first his mother and then his uncle bought cottages at the English Courtyard Association's development at Malthouse Court in Towcester. But he was now gracious enough to admit that he had been proved totally wrong and that it had been an enormous success for both of them! Indeed, so impressed had he become with the Association's work that, he told me, should a managerial position ever become available at ECA he would be delighted to have the opportunity to be considered.

Such an opportunity arose in 2007, and Christopher Mackenzie-Beevor joined the ECA Board as its Operations Director. His arrival provided the executive stability that the Board desperately needed, as well as wide experience in dealing with people at all levels. Christopher had had an extremely distinguished military career, during which he received the OBE, and later the CBE, for services to NATO. He became Colonel of his regiment, 1st The Queen's Dragoon Guards, and a Member of Her Majesty's Bodyguard of the Honourable Corps of the Gentleman at Arms. On retiring from the army he became a director of a conference equipment company. He proved a great addition to the Association and, in due course, my natural successor.

******

Grounds and Management

A main feature of the English Courtyard Association has always been our grounds. Indeed, the grounds have been as much an architectural feature of our developments as the buildings themselves so that they complement each other. Thus the Association's architects, the Sidell Gibson Partnership, have always been closely involved and ultimately responsible for their design. However, the Association also had its own landscape architects, the first being Ian Dougil of Athos Design. Ian set the standard that others were to follow, using interesting changes of level, and combining colour and variety which all residents love, whilst managing to achieve low maintenance costs. We were also lucky to have Tim Lynch, who took over from Ian and for many years became largely responsible for the design concept of our gardens and its execution. His landscaping schemes won many prizes for the Association. In fact, when we did a survey across residents and enquirers, 80% said a main reason for their move was 'the garden'.

The other major responsibility of the landscape architects was to ensure standards were maintained throughout the Association by overseeing the Courtyard Managers, offering advice, assistance and encouragement, and arranging for them to go on gardening courses, such as pruning and grass maintenance: for although the Courtyard Managers were enthusiastic and willing to learn, they were not necessarily expert gardeners at the outset. Their appointment was primarily for their caring and managerial roles, and only secondly for their gardening knowledge and ability.

Their other, equally important, task was communication with residents. Most residents had had large gardens of their own and many knew a lot about gardening. One of the main reasons why residents came to an English Courtyard was because they either could no longer look after their gardens themselves or were unable to find gardeners to look after them. For those who love their gardens there is nothing more depressing than seeing them going to rack and ruin because they can no longer maintain them.

Residents' allotments at South Petherton

St Luke's Court: flower beds

The opportunity to enjoy and, within reason, participate in the Association's gardens has always been important to residents, and the Association's design has made this possible. All cottages and ground floor flats have their own private patio garden, whilst residents also have the opportunity to take responsibility for the flower beds in front of their properties or – if they become too much for them to look after – to hand them back to the Courtyard Managers to maintain.

As the Association grew, the landscape architects that had been involved in the layout of the Association's developments were replaced by two part-time in-house landscape managers, who divided the responsibility for overseeing the maintenance of ECA's grounds between them. Their primary roles were to ensure that the standard of ECA's grounds was maintained, to advise and assist the Courtyard Managers, and to liaise with residents, answer their questions, seek their views and carry out their wishes whenever possible.

As with everything else that the English Courtyard Association provided, the grounds were provided for the benefit of the residents, not for the benefit of the management.

Chapter VI

Desmond Low, the Press, Guernsey and Foreign Climes

From the earliest days and for the following ten years, the English Courtyard Association was news. No one had ever before produced housing for the retired to their standard. Michael Hanson wrote in *Country Life* in 1987: '*Three* [Housing Design] *Awards, each in a different region of Britain, were won by the English Courtyard Association and its architects the Sidell Gibson Partnership. This has never been accomplished before by any developer or architects. It will be difficult to match, and well-nigh impossible to beat.*'

Whole-page articles and photographs appeared in the *Daily Telegraph*, the *Times*, the *Financial Times*, the *Sunday Times*, and the *Observer*. Magazines, including *Country Life*, *The Architect's Journal*, *The Architectural Review* and the magazines *Building*, *Home Finder* and *Moneycare*, published multi-page feature articles. Articles about the Association appeared in the publications of the Department of the Environment, National House Building Council and Royal Institute of British Architects Design Awards, as well as examples of the best of British architecture such as Crittles Court, Wadhurst and Walpole Court, Puddletown featuring in HRH the Prince of Wales' book *A Vision of Britain*.

National journalists wanted to meet those responsible and would travel as far as Torquay and Kent for an interview and to see at first hand what the Association was doing. The Association also had an excellent public relations consultant, the late Desmond Low, who knew all the leading property journalists personally and would arrange for me to meet them for lunch in convenient Fleet Street restaurants.

Those days are now virtually over. Few national newspapers have 'in-house' journalists any more, nor do journalists visit developments, so they rarely see for themselves what is being done or the standard of building being produced, preferring instead to rely on press releases or follow up residents' personal stories by telephone, rather than write about design. It is all part of the newspapers' current 'reality and celebrity' culture and due – in fairness to journalists – to their lack of time. But it makes press coverage much more difficult to achieve today. ECA's residents come to ECA for a quiet life. Understandably, on the whole, they are unhappy about reading about themselves and seeing their alleged comments quoted in a national newspaper!

So today good press coverage is difficult to obtain, and although advertising in the national press – depending on one's ability to afford it – still brings in enquiries and customers, most of the enquiries now come through the internet via the ECA website www.englishcourtyardassociation.org.uk

But in those early days press comment was hugely significant in bringing the Association to the attention of the British public. Not only did it bring in the majority of enquiries and purchasers for ECA properties, it brought offers of potential sites not only in the UK but also abroad.

The first of these that landed on my desk came from Guernsey, from Ken Rowe who had read an article in *Country Life*. Formerly a tomato grower, with the demise of Guernsey's tomato exports Rowe turned property speculator and acquired the White Woods Hotel, which was rather seedy but had about ten acres of ground in Castel, which Rowe thought could be ideal for an ECA development.

It sounded an interesting opportunity and a new challenge which, if successful, could lead to opportunities in Europe. It also gave Christopher the opportunity for some excellent sailing and to combine some business with pleasure! But first a new Guernsey company – Les Blancs Bois Ltd. – had to be formed, and special planning permission obtained so that the development could include both 'open market' and 'local market' properties.

Guernsey's housing regulations are unique. To avoid their small island being swamped by immigrants, strict restrictions are placed on those wishing to purchase property who come either from the UK mainland or from abroad. Immigration is controlled through a quota system. A limited number of houses are officially nominated as being 'open market', and only these houses may be purchased by those not of Guernsey birth. Usually these are the largest and most expensive houses in Guernsey, since their purchasers bring wealth to the island and create employment. It is in effect a method of taxation. All other housing is designated solely for 'local market' use. The system ensures that competition for housing from abroad cannot force up the price of local housing, and it works extremely well.

Christopher Thornhill persuaded the Guernsey government to grant planning permission for 44 self-contained apartments, 25% of which were to be 'open market' and 75% 'local market'. The properties were to be based on the traditional Guernsey farmhouse. Management, recruited locally initially, provided the normal ECA Courtyard Manager service, though this was relaxed by the Guernsey authorities over time. However, those buying 'open market' properties at Les Blancs Bois had to be already resident on the island. They could not come direct from the UK or abroad, and this remains the case today.

This meant that two identical properties – one 'local market' and the other 'open market' – could be sold at different prices, the 'open market' property frequently costing twice as much as the 'local market' one! But the system worked harmoniously and it was both understood and accepted by all who came to live at Les Blancs Bois, without hesitation and without any suggestion of there being a 'them and us'. It was the Robin Hood principle: the rich benefited the poor, or rather benefited the local islanders!

Another press introduction brought me in touch with the late Peter Laing, a retired soldier and fluent Spanish speaker, who knew Spain well. He had visited several ECA developments and was extremely enthusiastic about ECA developing properties in Spain. In particular, Peter knew of a site near Valderrama, Sotogrande, in southern Spain, that he thought would be ideal. I went with him to Spain to investigate.

It was indeed an excellent site, near the polo ground and the golf course of Valderrama, which over the next 25 years was to become a world famous golf course, home to the Volvo Masters and host to the Ryder Club. Undoubtedly, had it been pursued it would have been a great success, but developing in Spain required a Spanish partner, which ECA and its development partners did not have, and without the right Anglo-Spanish connections it seemed to be too big a gamble and a step too far.

Other expeditions to Faro in Portugal led to nothing. Then, just as Christopher and I were thinking of dropping our interest in Spain and Portugal, we were contacted by Charles Fairweather of Arnold Hill with a proposition which removed many of the concerns felt about Valderrama. Fairweather was handling the sale of land and property at Bendinat, a seaside village near Palma in Majorca, which was currently being developed as an exclusive golf course with villas and a club – the Anchorage Club – along the lines of the Marbella Club in Spain. But Fairweather assured us that there was more than sufficient land available for an ECA style development.

It just sounded as if Bendinat might be ideal, and an opportunity to launch an ECA flagship development in Europe. Desmond Low also knew of the development through his press contacts, so he and I arranged a visit. The development of Bendinat had commenced some two years earlier in 1986, and by the time Desmond and I arrived there the first nine holes of the golf course, the impressive Anchorage Club and a number of villas had already been completed to the highest standards, in an exotic Mediterranean style reminiscent of the Aga Khan's Costa Smeralda development and Prince Alfonso von Hohenlohe's model for Marbella, both clearly a major influence on the Bendinat development.

It was always envisaged that an ECA development at Bendinat would be multi-national, although the main market would be for the English. There were over a hundred thousand English people who had retired to Spain, many of whom had never learned the Spanish language, so problems arose when their health was threatened and hospital treatment required. For many the only option was to return to England to be treated, and frequently – if unwillingly – they had to remain there.

Being part of a largely English community at an ECA style development in Bendinat not only gave an English family – particularly if they were golf lovers – a luxurious life style in a warm seaside climate, it offered them the security that they lacked in Spain on their own, since obviously all ECA staff would need to be bilingual and able to deal with any emergency that arose, as well as setting up any medical links that were required.

The new venture looked extremely promising. George Steer and Christopher Thornhill joined me in Bendinat, and although George was paralyzed for three days with food poisoning (he seemed to have forgotten that he was allergic to mussels!), we were all enthusiastic about what we saw. Progress was made, and two possible sites for an ECA style development were identified.

But by the end of August 1989 everything had changed. House prices had been rising at an ever-increasing rate and the British government was becoming worried. They took the decision to end multi-mortgage ownership, a system whereby several students or young purchasers could band together to buy a house in order to get on to the property ladder. It seemed an excellent idea but, once revoked, it was never renewed, resulting in the average age of a first time buyer in 2011 being 37! The end of multi-mortgage ownership was the trigger that began the property crash that continued for the next three to four years.

The English Courtyard Association was particularly vulnerable as they had three developments in Somerset being built consecutively, all within a radius of 15 miles of each other, at South Petherton, Taunton and Ilminster. Although the South Petherton development had been completed and the first purchasers at Taunton were in residence – and despite all ECA's developments in Somerset being amongst their very best and situated in delightful locations – sales were severely hit. Many potential purchasers could no longer sell their own houses easily, and others who really did not need to move immediately postponed putting their homes on the market until the property market had recovered. Certainly it was a lesson to ECA for the future. They would be wise to build and market only one ECA development – in the same county – at a time.

Sadly, the recession killed any possibility of proceeding with the Bendinat project, and by 1994, when the property market had recovered, there was no longer the will or the enthusiasm to try again.

Chapter VII

Financial Developments

For centuries, and certainly during the 40 years covering the birth of my 'idea', property and financial markets witnessed the crest of a wave repeatedly followed by a trough. Heady days when property developers and banks experienced nothing but ever- increasing sales and profits were followed, as surely as night follows day, by the collapse of both, resulting in falling profits, squeezed liquidity, falling house prices and stagnant house sales.

During this period many banks and property companies overstretched themselves in their enthusiasm to lend and borrow money against property. This resulted in over-borrowing or over-lending, which led in turn to fringe banks and property companies having neither sufficient security to finance their loans or resources to cover their debts. Like all other organizations involved in the property and financial fields, in order to survive the crisis and weather the storm ECA needed to improvise and to introduce financial mechanisms to help resolve their problem.

In the late 1970s, mortgages for the retired did not exist. But with the rapid increase in house prices in the early 1980s mortgages were now becoming essential, not just for the young (for whom they had been available for many years, usually on a capital-plus-interest repayment basis spread over 25 years), but also for the elderly.

Sir William Tweddle, Chairman of the Leeds Permanent Building Society, was also my mother's solicitor. I suggested to him that there was a requirement for interest-only mortgages, a system whereby interest on the mortgage would be repaid monthly whilst repayment of the capital on the outstanding loan would be deferred until either the death of the borrower or the sale of the property.

Although this suggestion was not taken up by the Leeds, the proposal was approved and accepted by the Nationwide Building Society's Cheltenham office, and interest-only mortgages were born.

It is worth recording that, by the time the English Courtyard Association completed its third development at Crittles Court, Wadhurst, some 25% of ECA's purchasers were taking advantage of interest-only mortgages.

Part of the demand for interest-only mortgages stemmed from the steep increase in house prices. These had risen by 25% in the three years since the completion of Manor Court, Pewsey. During this time I was receiving numbers of letters from would-be purchasers on the mailing list, regretfully explaining that, having visited an English Courtyard Association development and liked the concept enormously, they much regretted that they could no longer afford the increased prices and requested that their names be removed from the mailing list.

But overall the property market at the time was buoyant, and Crittles Court proved a great success and was very well received.

It was not until 1985/6 – coinciding with the creation of the ECA's first, and only, small development of nine cottages at Hassels Courtyard, Long Melford – that the effect of property market recession hit the Association. ECA faced two main problems at Hassels Court: first, the recession in the property market itself, and second, the relatively high cost of ECA's service charge.

Many of the costs that make up the service charge remain constant, irrespective of whether a development is being built to service nine properties or 25. But the charge to residents varies appreciably depending on the number of properties in each development. This – as in the case of Hassels Courtyard – is because the total service cost has to be divided between nine properties as opposed to a norm of 25. Consequently the smaller the development (providing the services offered are exactly the same) the higher the service charge.

These two factors, occurring as they did at the same time, caused a sales problem and with it the need for the development company to offer its first shared-equity scheme.

Shared equity had to be used with discretion; it was not possible for us to offer it to everyone. The development company's role is to develop, not to finance the purchase of residents' properties. So this method of funding the purchase was only used to help those purchasers whom the Association knew really wanted to come to Hassels Courtyard but genuinely felt they could not afford the asking price. In such cases the development company left a percentage of the sales price outstanding – usually up to 25% – and took a charge on the cottage. The development company then took that same percentage of the sales proceeds when the property was later resold in 5-25 years' time.

These types of shared-equity schemes, over the years, were used by property companies nationwide, particularly in times of recession. The idea was good, but care needed to be taken by those using such schemes to ensure that they were fair both to the purchaser and to the organization financing the purchase. In such cases the services of an independent financial adviser are always recommended.

In 1987 the English Courtyard Association was marketing Hildesley Court in East Ilsley, when a national scheme was launched by the Rosehaugh Group to assist the purchasers of 'sheltered housing' (a rather unfortunate generic term used to describe managed retirement housing in both the private and public sectors). The scheme, which Rosehaugh pioneered with great success, was called Home for Life.

The Home for Life Plan provided an additional option for those wishing to buy a purpose-built and managed retirement property. It enabled purchasers, if they so wished, to buy a life lease, instead of purchasing the property outright. In any market this could be an advantage, but in a difficult housing market it was particularly helpful. It allowed those who either were unable to afford, or unwilling to pay, the full builder's price to purchase a life lease which gave them the same security of tenure as a freehold or long lease, but at a much reduced price. The actual amount payable depended upon whether the property was for single or married occupancy, and the projected age expectancy of the purchasers.

Examples in the Home for Life literature, at this time, showed that a man age 81 and his wife aged 78 would receive a contribution from Home for Life of 42.5% of the purchase price of a life lease. A single man aged 81 would receive a contribution from Home for Life of 58.5% and a single woman aged 78 would receive 47.9%.

Opportunities also existed for a shared equity option, but in the majority of cases – where children's interests were not involved – under the lease the ownership of the property reverted to Home for Life on the death of the last occupant. Indeed the only real downside was the effect it could have on the children, who could see that their inheritance could be affected, as they would receive little or nothing from the sale of their parents' property. However, the advantage to their parents could be substantial. Their security would be guaranteed; they would be able to pay appreciably less for the property than its market value; and in many cases they would be left with more disposable income than would otherwise have been the case. Also in some cases inheritance tax would be saved from the parents' estate. But Rosehaugh was an ethical organization and took great care to ensure that children were always made fully aware of how a life lease could affect them.

Sadly, Rosehaugh was forced to discontinue the scheme after only a few years of its operation. For a number of purchasers it was an extremely good and fair scheme. It had proved itself to be beneficial to many purchasers in their retirement, and it was taken up by 15-20% of the purchasers at Hildesley Court. But unfortunately the bulk of Rosehaugh's sheltered housing property portfolio consisted of low-priced sheltered housing. These properties, unlike English Courtyard Association properties, failed to increase in value sufficiently to warrant further investment, and the scheme was discontinued.

Nonetheless the Home for Life service to the retirement industry is well worth being studied by other financial institutions. Undoubtedly there is still a serious need for such a service.

It is perhaps worth adding a postscript. Historically, English Courtyard Association properties have always out-performed the market in a recession. In 1991 the property market was in the depths of its first serious crash since the war. For the benefit of potential purchasers and English Courtyard Association residents, the Association – assisted by the Courtyard Managers, a number of residents and the journalist and television personality and interviewer Libby Purves – produced a video. The video explained that during the years 1981 to 1991 there were 70 resales of ECA properties and that the average ECA resale outperformed the property market throughout that period by over 2.5%.

During the whole period of the recession which ran from August 1989 until 1994, although sales took longer to achieve prices of ECA properties largely kept their value. This, in part, was because the purchase of an ECA property is often needs-driven; whilst the vendor of an ordinary property may prefer to wait until the property market has recovered. A purchaser who needs the security of an ECA development often can-not afford to do so.

It is also worth mentioning that, particularly in a recession, estate agents tend to reduce house prices substantially in order to achieve a sale, sometimes at almost any price. They use the same criteria when valuing an ECA property as they would for valuing any other similar-sized property. The use of estate agents for the sale of ECA properties can therefore drive ECA house prices down unnecessarily, so *caveat vendor*!

The situation in 2010/2012 may not be exactly the same as in 1991, but there are certainly parallels to be drawn between the two.

Chapter VIII

ECA and the Hungerford Site

By 1981, Paul Greenwood, at this time a local partner/director in John D Wood, was beginning to feel disenchanted with his involvement with the English Courtyard Association. Since before its formation Paul had been invaluable to both Christopher and myself. He had supported me and my Big Idea from the outset, when it was still a dream. He had allowed me free office space over an extended period, whilst ECA was getting off the ground. He had introduced me to Christopher Thornhill and, through him, to the financial investment provided by the Bonas Group. Together he and I had fronted the sales effort at Manor Court from John D Wood's Newbury offices, with great success. Indeed, Paul had played a key role in the whole Manor Court success story which, because it was a totally different concept and type of development from anything that had preceded it, had attracted huge press coverage.

However, from the commencement of ECA's second development at Berrow Court, Upton-upon-Severn, it became clear that John D Wood would have the utmost difficulty in servicing the sales need at Upton-upon-Severn, and from then on Paul's close involvement with ECA began to decline.

In the early and mid-1970s, Paul's office in Newbury was over an hour's drive from Upton-upon-Severn. John D Wood's other offices in the Upton area were equally distant. It was therefore virtually impossible for John D Wood to undertake a major sales operation in that area, let alone supply sales staff for the site. Furthermore, the property market was now in a severe recession. Fringe banks were failing and interest rates were sky-high, well into double figures and going higher. Through no fault of his own, Paul's ability to contribute to Berrow Court was becoming minimal.

This inevitably led to Christopher and myself – and myself in particular – taking an ever-increasing role in the sales operation. This entailed taking over national and local advertising, using local estate agencies on a 'winner take all' basis (if the agency introduced a purchaser who bought an ECA property at Berrow Court, they would automatically receive the full 2% commission), carrying out a massive PR campaign brilliantly orchestrated by Desmond Low, and the appointment of the Courtyard Manager, Derek Hazelwood, as my assistant, in order to provide much needed sales representation on the ground since he lived on the development.

ECA were also able to use their guest suite in the sales process, and I frequently based myself there for two or three nights per week. The guest suite could also be used by potential purchasers, particularly those that had come any distance. Many purchasers liked to stay overnight, to acclimatize themselves and get a flavour of life on an ECA development, and to meet other residents who had already moved in, who because of their enthusiasm for Berrow Court made far and away the best and most effective sales force!

As this could be organized on all future sites by ECA, the need for Paul Greenwood's involvement became peripheral, unless ECA had a site near a John D Wood office.

Meanwhile Paul, together with his assistant Guy Mossop, organized a merger with local Reading estate agents Martin and Pole. Together they founded Martin & Pole John D Wood.

In 1985 Paul Greenwood was offered a district partnership in Knight, Frank & Rutley (as it was then called) based in their Hungerford office. Paul asked Christopher Thornhill if he could take the ECA business with him to Knight, Frank & Rutley, who were – and still remain – the UK's most prestigious estate agency. This was refused. ECA had decided that they could not commit themselves to any specific outside agency. It was better for them to control and service all ECA's sales themselves, using John D Wood, Knight Frank & Rutley or any other estate agent as appropriate, paying them commission on a 'winner take all' basis and also paying them a substantial finder's fee if they introduced a suitable site, and one which ECA's development company partners, Geometer Developments, were prepared to purchase for them.

Needless to say Paul was unhappy with this arrangement. He felt that it would have been a feather in his cap if he were able to bring the ECA account with him to KFR. At that time ECA and their development company were the best known developers and managers of luxury retirement property in the country, having already won many top architectural awards, and Paul understandably felt that he had been partially instrumental in creating its reputation – which indeed he certainly had.

Between them, Paul and Guy Mossop had introduced ECA to sites at Lyefield Court, Emmer Green, near Reading, at Atwater Court, Lenham, in Kent, and at Hildesley Court, East Ilsey, near Newbury, as well as to a number of other sites that neither ECA nor our development company wished to pursue. Paul and Guy knew exactly the sort of site that would be ideal for an ECA development. Those that they had introduced to ECA had all been successful, although the charming racing village of East Ilsey lost some of its appeal when the village lost both its shop and local post office. They also understood ECA's market and management structure.

By 1985 Paul was established in KFR's Hungerford office, whilst Guy Mossop remained with Martin & Pole John D Wood in Reading. It was then that Guy learned of a superb site – ideal for a luxury retirement development – on the A4 in Hungerford. He knew the owners of the site personally, and suggested to us that it would be a perfect site for an ECA development.

It was indeed a superb site and a fabulous location, almost adjoining the well-known Bear Hotel, and I, particularly, was extremely keen that Geometer Developments should purchase it. But Christopher, with input from Stephen Alexander, the development company's accountant, considered the site too close to the A4, and that the river running through it and the lake could well incur unforeseen costs at the development stage and later for the management. When all the sums were complete, the site was considered to be too expensive to develop. After almost a year of prevarication, to my great disappointment the site was turned down.

By now Guy Mossop had met Henry Thornton, the young and very talented director of a building company with an extremely good reputation, and suggested that they should develop the Hungerford site together. Terms having been agreed between them, Guy met up with Paul Greenwood and informed him that he wanted to build an 'exact copy' of an English Courtyard Association development.

Paul, Knight Frank & Rutley and Guy Mossop were to handle the sales. Henry Thornton, as the developer, was to be both Chairman and Managing Director of the new development company, Beechcroft Developments. They also formed a non-profit making management company, the Beechcroft Trust, on similar lines to ECA. In due course, Paul Greenwood also became Chairman of the Beechcroft Trust.

Bearwater, as the development was named, was set in some five acres of attractive grounds, with a lake and a private pathway to Hungerford High Street. Its

Bearwater: The Beechcroft development at Hungerford

spacious red-brick houses and flats, impressive but slightly austere, reminiscent in architectural style of one of Norman Foster's Knightsbridge developments, surrounded a courtyard divided by an office and a block of flats. Garages backed on to the A4 to reduce the noise of passing traffic. The design and format were all too familiar to Christopher and me! Nonetheless it was an excellent development, very successful and well received.

The only real difference between ECA and BT lay in the service that the Trust offered. BT provided only one on-site manager or 'Resident Secretary', usually a woman, whose official office hours were three hours a day, 9 am-12 pm, five days per week. The Resident Secretary or her deputy provided reduced emergency cover over week-ends. Approximately half of BT's developments had no living-in accommodation for staff, which meant that many of their Secretaries lived off-site. None of their sites had a guest suite, laundry or minibus service for their residents. But their developments had excellent grounds, and a few had swimming pools and tennis courts, with the aim of appealing to a younger market, thus highlighting their philosophy of 'independent living' rather than ECA's philosophy of providing buildings designed specifically to service the needs of all those 'from early retirement onwards'.

The English Courtyard Association from the outset had always recognized, perhaps more consciously than the Beechcroft Trust, that as time progressed younger residents became older residents, and their needs changed. ECA's buildings and services had always reflected this. However, a major advantage for BT purchasers was that BT's service charge was inevitably less expensive!

Initially I was furious – Beechcroft's Hungerford development was, in my view, total plagiarism. However, after a while, reason prevailed and I had to acknowledge and accept that Paul, who had given me so much assistance when forming ECA, had every right to use his knowledge of ECA to both his own and Beechcroft's advantage. It was, after all, impossible to patent an idea, and – as the saying goes – 'imitation is the sincerest form of flattery'! Paul and Guy had given Christopher and myself every opportunity to purchase the Hungerford site, and we had turned the opportunity down!

Suffice it to say that the Bearwater development scheme was a great success, and Beechcroft emerged as the first – probably the only – true competitor to the English Courtyard Association, providing similar spacious and attractive retirement housing. Since then – and for well over 20 years – the two companies have been friendly rivals, competing in similar markets. Many purchasers used to make their decision to purchase based upon whichever location suited them the best, whilst others made their decision based upon the organization whose service best suited their needs.

When a merger of the managements of the English Courtyard Association and the Beechcroft Trust was agreed and eventually completed in 2010, under the Cognatum banner, (Cognatum means bringing together), the merger guaranteed the retention of the name, service and ethos of the two organizations.

Paul Greenwood could claim with justification to be – if not the father – certainly the godfather of both!

Chapter IX

The Concept

The English Courtyard Association is dedicated to providing specialised luxury accommodation for elderly and retired people. The concept of English Courtyard's developments is based on:

- *The need for comfortable, spacious living accommodation in a pleasant setting near to shops and other facilities*

- *The need to combine complete independence and privacy with the security of someone to call on in an emergency*

- *The need to take into account the physical problems of advancing age*

- *The need to protect fixed incomes and capital against inflation*

To achieve this, the Association promotes a very high standard of building by private developers, especially designed to meet the needs of elderly people. When a development is complete and occupied the Association takes it over and manages it on a non-profit making basis for the benefit of the residents.

Each development includes accommodation for 2 full time resident Courtyard Managers (normally a husband and wife team) whose duty is to answer alarm calls, ensure a high standard of management and maintenance of the grounds, give advice and help in any emergency.

The cottages and flats are normally for sale on long leases of 150 years. The occupier, but not necessarily the owner, has to be a person of retirement age.

The cottages and flats are sold at property market prices and the owners' capital will increase/decrease in line with the general inflation in property prices and the market conditions.

The running cost – the service charge – is kept as low as reasonably possible – whilst ensuring the standards of the Association are properly maintained, thus giving a certain amount of protection against inflation for those on fixed incomes.

The inspiration for the English Courtyard Association came from Noel Shuttleworth. Searching for accommodation for his elderly mother he found a complete lack of any place that combined a background of security and emergency help with a running cost that could be met from a modest fixed income and with a reasonable hedge against inflation for limited capital.

In Geometer Developments, Shuttleworth found a private development company that enjoys operating in specialised and "difficult" markets and which welcomes the opportunity of building to a standard that is not usually justified by purely commercial considerations.

When the cottages and flats are all sold, the freehold of each development is passed to the English Courtyard Association, the developer's profit is released and thereafter the scheme is managed on a non-profit making basis. This ensures that the original design and purpose for the development are properly protected, in the best interest of the residents.

English Courtyard Association developments are based on the traditional courtyard plan of almshouses and consist of terraces and courts of two storey cottages and a few flats.

The style of the buildings blends with the architecture of the district and traditional local materials are used whenever possible. The English Courtyard Association tries to combine the best of the old and the new (e.g. locally made bricks, stone-mullioned windows, modern standard of domestic luxury and VHF alarm systems).

The grounds are landscaped to create the relaxed atmosphere of the garden of a country house or an Oxford College. The Association looks after the grounds and the main structure of the buildings (external maintenance, roofs, gutters etc) but the residents retain control of their own domestic expenditure.

Developments are sited close to the centre of attractive market towns or large villages, within easy walking distance of shops, so that residents are not cut off without a car.

English Courtyard Association developments provide a complete home from early retirement onwards for people who are worried about living alone or are finding the management of a house or garden is becoming a burden.

The houses are designed with many special features to take into account residents' potential needs and advancing age (e.g. alarm system, wheelchair access, ability to live on one floor — substantial storage space in the loft) enabling residents to lead a comfortable and active life in their own home long after they would have to leave an ordinary house. There is also a convenient laundry available on the development and a comfortable guest suite where friends and family may come and stay.

******

The concept and aims of the Association, as they appear above, were written in July 1979 and issued, along with the original Manor Court, Pewsey brochure, to all potential purchasers. These have never changed and are as true and appropriate today, as the day on which the Association was founded. One point that cannot be emphasized enough — as it is so extremely important — is that, although the buildings are financed with commercial monies, the Association itself is entirely non-profit making. It exists solely in order to serve the best interests of its residents, for whom all its buildings were built. The leasehold system used is a protection for residents. It prevents those that come later changing the external architectural design of the buildings without the agreement of the Association and, since there are no shareholders in the Association, no one but the residents can profit from the sale of any of its buildings.

The idea of providing services for the elderly, and trying to make a profit out of the service, must be seriously questioned. There is quite clearly a conflict of interest. Which becomes the more important – the profit or the service? Two of the largest national providers and managers of both sheltered housing and nursing homes have recently both got themselves into severe financial difficulties by trying to make a profit out of their services. If either is to survive they will either require a Government bailout or need to cut their staff – and thus the service that they provide – drastically. The consequences both to the taxpayer and to those receiving the care are quite unacceptable.

It should be reassuring to all lease-holders of English Courtyard Association properties that the Association's and their own financial position is secure, and that the service they receive remains assured.

Chapter X

The Properties

Up until the late 1970s the main providers of purpose-built properties for the retired were local councils. These were largely, blocks of one-bedroom flats to rent situated in urban areas. The English Courtyard Association not only brought purpose-built retirement housing for sale to market towns and rural areas but, with their architects, revolutionized the construction of retirement housing in the private sector, in the process changing public perception from one of institutionalized living to one offering independence, security and style. The design and architecture of its buildings and the creation of its beautifully landscaped grounds gave its residents an opportunity to retain, on a smaller scale, a gracious way of life with dignity, freedom and respect in their retirement.

Gracious retirement homes

Architecture and Design

Although I may have had the idea, it was Paul Gibson, Giles Downes and later Richard Morton of the Sidell Gibson Partnership who transformed the idea into design, and Christopher Thornhill who so skilfully implemented the construction of the buildings. Together we made a major impact on the house building industry, and a great many imitators followed in our wake. For fifteen years, from 1978 to 1993, ECA led the field in championing housing for the retired, combining innovative design with traditional facades which merged with their environment, to produce the best accommodation of its type.

During this period, the Association and its architects won nine of the most prestigious of all architectural and design awards, presented jointly by the Minister of Housing and Construction, the Chairman of the National House Building Council and the President of the Royal Institute of British Architects. It also won four Civic Trust commendations. Unlike today, these were not just industry awards for sheltered housing, they were the cream of national awards, open to all comers in the house building industry and to every type of development.

Cottages

Manor Court, Pewsey

The traditional two-bedroom cottage is the standard-bearer for all English Courtyard Association properties. It changed the perceived idea of retirement living and brought it back to its roots. As mentioned previously, the decision arose when visiting an elderly resident at the beautiful Elizabethan almshouses at Froxfield. On being asked whether she found stairs difficult, she vehemently assured us that she would always go upstairs to bed, if it took the last breath in her body to do so. From that, the cottage concept was born. The ECA cottage was designed to offer sufficient space for most couples' needs, bearing in mind that residents also have what is effectively a third bedroom – the use of a comfortable self-contained guest suite, where friends and family can come and stay for up to five days at a time, if booked in advance, and at minimal cost.

The cottage is about flexibility, about early retirement onwards, about good-sized rooms. It consists of two proper double bedrooms, an en-suite bathroom and an airing cupboard upstairs, above which there is a loft, with substantial storage space, reached by a loft ladder. Downstairs there is an entrance hall, sitting room, dining room, kitchen, cloakroom with shower (or bath) and a patio garden (many cottages also have sun rooms or conservatories).

The cottage takes into account that a young retired couple may wish to enjoy a life of travel, or visits to family and friends, and that they can do so knowing that their property is secure and without having to worry about looking after a garden, or the maintenance of their home, whilst they are away.

It is also designed to take into account a resident's dignity and the problems that can occur with advancing age. The stairs are straight and a stair-lift can be easily installed. A full wheelchair lift can also be installed from the rear corner of the sitting room to the rear bedroom. Sockets are placed at a convenient height. Lever taps take into account the threat of arthritis. A cupboard at the back of the bath doubles as a potentially useful seat. The walls of the bathroom have strong points where grab-rails and bath hoists may be installed if required. Every attempt has been made to ensure easy access to cupboards, drawers and cooking units, and the whole ground floor can be transformed with ease into a self-contained flat, with a bedroom, sitting room, shower room, kitchen and patio garden, whilst the upstairs rooms could, if necessary, be used for living-in staff. But most importantly it retains, both externally and internally, the appearance of a charming traditional two-bedroom cottage.

Apartments

Historically, many people in retirement prefer living on one floor. Therefore, from the outset ECA provided apartments. Apart from a single one-bedroom flat at Manor Court, Pewsey, and three in the conversion of Fullands House at Taunton where space dictated otherwise, all apartments contain a minimum of two bedrooms, on the basis that couples may each need their own bedroom. The standard design for an apartment includes a sitting/dining room which can be sub-divided as required, a large double bedroom with en-suite bathroom, a second double bedroom, a shower room, storage cupboards and a kitchen.

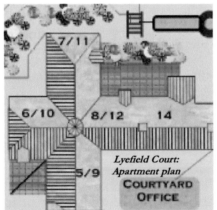

Lyefield Court: Apartment plan

It was not until the Association's fourth development at Lyefield Court, Emmer Green, that ECA produced a development where the majority of properties were apartments, the idea being that, as Lyefield Court was on the outskirts of Reading, a major town, purchasers might be more used to apartment living and the additional security that this provides. Therefore 16 apartments were built in two groups of eight, each group in the shape of a cross, at the centre of which, beneath an impressive dome, was an entrance hall, from which led four apartments on each floor, those on the first floor being serviced by a grand staircase, fitted with a stair-lift. The importance of this design was that not only did it allow for light and airy apartments, but all 16 apartments were able to enjoy views over the grounds on two sides, and eight of them views on three sides. Ground floor apartments had a small garden, whilst those on the first floor enjoyed French windows leading onto a covered balcony. This excellent innovative design influenced apartment construction on other ECA developments.

The Vinery, Torquay

Today the Association owns four purpose-built, all-apartment developments. The Vinery in Torquay is a magnificent Palladian building of two- and three-bedroom apartments built into a cliff. The design matches the finest classical traditions of the town. The development also boasts an attractive roof garden and conservatory, from which residents enjoy spectacular views over Torbay.

Wyke Mark is a luxurious three-storey building constructed in the shape of a horseshoe, set in an attractive wooded Winchester suburb.

Sandbourne Court, an elegant cliff-top development in a fashionable residential area of Bournemouth, overlooking Alum Chine is only a short walk from the shops and the sea.

Apartments at Wyke Mark

Apartments at Les Blancs Bois

Les Blancs Bois is a collegiate-style development of 44 self-contained apartments in Castel, Guernsey, set in beautiful mature grounds. The design is based on the traditional Guernsey farmhouse. Sadly, under Guernsey law, this development is only available to those already living on the Island, not to those living in the UK or elsewhere.

Maisonettes

For several years ECA purchasers had been requesting us to build some larger properties. The first of these were six large maisonettes at Framers Court, Lane End, integrated into the second level of the two apartment blocks. These were, and still are, extremely popular. But

Maisonettes at Framers Court

maisonettes are best suited to a site with two or more levels. What was needed, therefore, was a design that could easily be incorporated into a standard courtyard.

Wing Houses

The Manor House look

The 'wing house' was first introduced in 1998 in the second phase of Mytchett Heath. It was the brain child of Giles Downes of Sidell Gibson. Giles, who had worked on ECA projects since they began, received a CVO for his work on the restoration of the roof of St. George's Hall at Windsor Castle, following the fire of 1992. Giles came up with a most interesting, innovative and flexible design. This allowed two 'wing houses' to stand like book ends, with a standard ECA cottage between them, giving the impression of a small manor house with two wings. It also allowed for a number of other variations to this theme, since it fitted in so easily into the Courtyard model. It could also, if appropriate, incorporate an integral garage, which a number of purchasers appreciated.

The Wing House

Internally the wing house provided the Association with the size of rooms, flexibility space and design that we required. A hallway, off which was a cloakroom and cloak cupboard, led into a large L-shaped open plan room that could be divided into a separate drawing and dining room if preferred, off which were a large kitchen/diner, a double bedroom, a conservatory and a delightful patio garden. A staircase from the hall led into a pleasant open plan study/sitting room/third bedroom (as required) on the first floor, beyond which were a large bathroom and large, light double bedroom. This really spacious house allowed for downstairs living as, when and if required, with ample space for living-in staff. It also allowed for a younger retired couple to live in the house, with their elderly parent in the downstairs bedroom, safe in the knowledge that ECA's Courtyard Managers would be there to keep an eye and help, should an emergency occur whilst they were away.

Three-bedroom properties

After listening to purchasers' requests for larger properties, it was at the Association's third development, at Crittles Court, Wadhurst, that the decision was first taken to include several three- bedroom properties on the Courtyard. From 1982 onwards some three-bedroom properties, or properties with an additional study, became an option on all Courtyards.

Church Place, Ickenham: A third bedroom is over the archway

Four-bedroom properties

Lyefield Court: The four bedroom house

It was during a tour of Crittles Court that two potential purchasers approached me with a request. They liked what they had seen and were aware that the Association was planning to build our next development at Lyefield Court, Emmer Green, near Reading, close to where their family lived. But they wanted a larger property that allowed each of them more privacy.

The way to achieve this was for them to buy two adjoining properties, where the drawing room and dining room of both properties shared a common wall. This allowed the wall between the two drawing rooms to be removed and for them to have a four-bedroom house which provided them with one large drawing room, a dining room, a downstairs study, a kitchen and a pantry. Husband and wife each had their own entrance, and their own suite of bedroom, bathroom and sitting room upstairs. This not only met their requirements admirably, but it showed how the flexibility of the courtyard design could service a wide range of needs and tastes.

It was not the only time this was done. Sometime later, two neighbours at Lyefield Court got married and joined their two properties into one, whilst at Manor Court, Pewsey, two properties were joined together to make a four-bedroom property in order to provide accommodation for a live-in carer, as the lady was bedridden.

Other additions and variations to the Association's purpose-built courtyard accommodation over time included conservatories and garden rooms (which first appeared at Lyefield Court), sun rooms, the provision of the Courtyard's own minibus, a few double garages, and the introduction of the Association's first – and only – small development of nine cottages. This has not been repeated due to the effect it has on the service charge.

Interiors

How tall is your mother?

This question was once asked by a resident at Manor Court, who was delighted that she could reach all the cupboards and shelves, as well as the lowest electric switches, with consummate ease! Internal design of ECA properties is important, and needs to meet the requirements of residents as they grow older. It is as important, if not more so, as the facade and surroundings, and has received every bit as much attention from our architects. Internal design has always concentrated on space and flexibility. All two-floor properties provide modern kitchens, a minimum of two bath/shower rooms, one of them downstairs, additional loft-storage space, deep cupboards, a small private patio garden, and the ability to live on one floor, with live-in help if required.

A private patio garden

The less mobile can add a stair-lift, insert a full wheelchair lift from the dining room to the main bedroom, benefit from extra-wide doors for wheel access to all rooms, and find electric sockets at a convenient height. They can also insert a range of support rails and other aids in the bathrooms or elsewhere, to suit their needs, should these be necessary. The apartments are equally impressive. One of the joys of ECA properties is that whilst offering luxury and style they take into account advancing age, without ever appearing institutional. However, it is worth emphasizing that the interiors are built to mobility standards, and while they may not be suitable for every kind of severe disability they can also offer, in the right circumstances, an ideal solution to independent living for disabled people. From the outset interiors were designed with great thought and to the highest specifications, as these bird's-eye plans from the original Manor Court brochure of the kitchen, bathroom and downstairs cloakroom show.

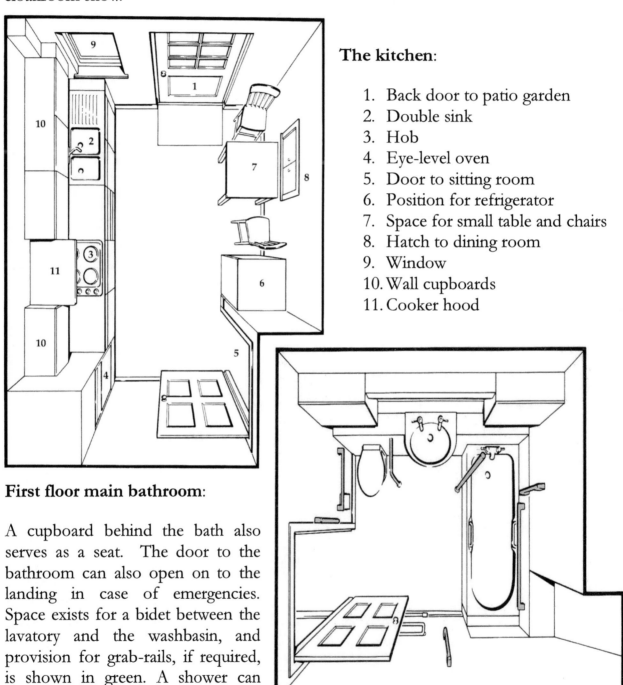

The kitchen:

1. Back door to patio garden
2. Double sink
3. Hob
4. Eye-level oven
5. Door to sitting room
6. Position for refrigerator
7. Space for small table and chairs
8. Hatch to dining room
9. Window
10. Wall cupboards
11. Cooker hood

First floor main bathroom:

A cupboard behind the bath also serves as a seat. The door to the bathroom can also open on to the landing in case of emergencies. Space exists for a bidet between the lavatory and the washbasin, and provision for grab-rails, if required, is shown in green. A shower can also be fitted above the bath.

The downstairs cloakroom

The downstairs cloakroom allows anyone, if necessary, to live on the ground floor. The suite of rooms above can then become available for living-in staff or help. Positions available for grab-rails are depicted in green. The cloakroom offers three design layout options:

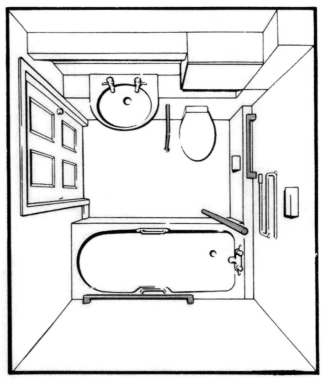

A bathroom

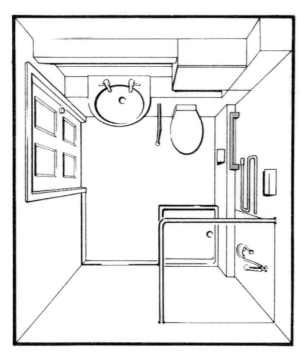

A cloakroom with shower

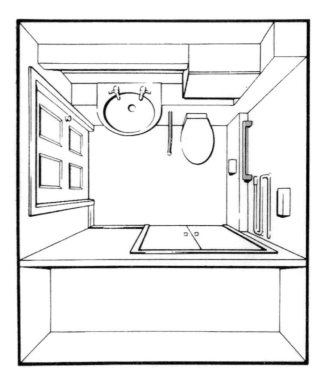

A cloakroom with a large cloak cupboard

59

Cottage interior from the dining room

Cottage kitchen

Cottage bedroom

Apartment interior

Ensuite bathroom

Wing house interior

Chapter XI

Index of services common to most Courtyards from 1979 to 1990

- Two resident Courtyard Managers – usually a husband and wife team – on duty five days per week

- A Relief Manager to provide cover when Courtyard Managers are off duty or on holiday

- 24-hour emergency cover

- Aid Call or Tunstall Alarm system installed

- On-site laundry

- Self-contained guest suite available for residents' guests

- A garage for each property

- Visitor parking

- All cottages and ground floor apartments have their own private patio garden

- Allotment areas are available at most developments

Services and facilities added to most developments after 1990

- Minibus (provided at 17 Courtyards)

- CCTV security surveillance systems

Allotments in Walled Garden at Lenham

Chapter XII

The Very First Courtyard, Manor Court, 1978

Swan Road, Pewsey, Wiltshire SN9 5DW

Pewsey, on the Kennet and Avon Canal, is a large thriving rural village, with a wide range of shops for everyday needs. Its own railway station provides both a gateway to the West Country and a fast commuter service to London, Paddington. It is just over an hour's drive to Heathrow. The attractive market town of Marlborough is seven miles to the north and the cathedral city of Salisbury 21 miles to the south.

The sundial

King Alfred's statue stands in the centre of the village. King Alfred was a frequent visitor and during his campaigns he entrusted his wife to the care of the people of Pewsey. In gratitude and to celebrate his victories against the Danes he granted a day's holiday to the inhabitants. This is still commemorated each year by the colourful Pewsey Carnival.

Noel Shuttleworth's mother

Manor Court, the first English Courtyard Association development designed by Paul Gibson of the Sidell Gibson Partnership, was strongly influenced by the beautiful Elizabethan almshouses of nearby Froxfield. Built in 1978 of warm red local brick and clay tile with traditional stone mullioned windows, it stands in the shade of the medieval church and manor house. A sundial situated in the centre of the grounds commemorates my mother, who died just prior to the completion of the courtyard.

Woodland and riverside walk, Manor Court

Manor Court stands in 3½ acres of landscaped grounds. A footbridge leads to a woodland walk along the banks of the river Avon. Twenty cottages and four flats surround three sides of a courtyard. Each cottage contains two bedrooms and a bathroom upstairs, and a sitting room, dining room, kitchen and cloak/shower room downstairs, and has substantial additional storage space in the attic. A garage for most properties is nearby. There are also three two-bedroom apartments and a one-bedroom apartment, and a comfortable guest suite.

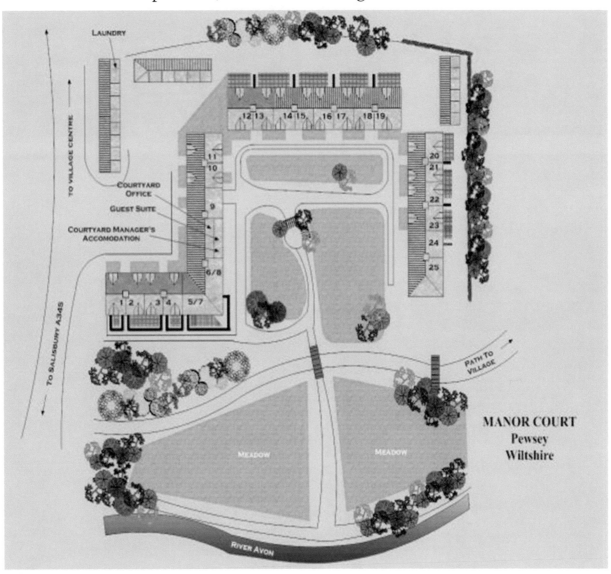

Chapter XIII

Press comments about Manor Court: Articles from Courtyard Views

'A new venture in an almost deserted part of the housing market is being launched this week by a group that describes itself as The English Courtyard Association. The association is an elegant title to describe an operation which older house buyers have been awaiting for years; top quality, compact, low-maintenance cottages for retired folk.'

COURTYARD FOCUS

Rolling back
the years

So began Jeremy Gates' Property File column in the *Daily Express* on 17 July 1979. Some months later the first residents moved into Manor Court, a picturesque development on the banks of the river Avon in the Wiltshire village of Pewsey. Now, 25 years on, the Association manages almost 900 properties in 33 locations across 20 English counties. Over the years the English Courtyard name has become synonymous with the very best in retirement housing.

The external appearance of an English Courtyard scheme and the high standards of landscaping and maintenance are timeless, but internally properties have evolved in subtle response to customer feedback and market trends. Satellite TV connections, under-floor heating, patented flush shower trays, duplex apartments, choices in kitchen and bathroom finishes – the specification is continually under review and the range of customer options increasing.

One thing which won't change, however, is English Courtyard's on-going belief in and commitment to the values and philosophy which underpinned the founders' original concept, namely:

• The creation of spacious, specially designed properties and gardens capable of adapting to meet the progressive needs and aspirations of older people.

• The achievement of a standard of design and construction that protects capital investment in the property for residents and their heirs.

• The protection of residents' fixed incomes against inflation and spiralling costs by careful, sympathetic and economic management – so far as it is possible.

The words may change a little, but their meaning is as valid today as it was back then.

Setting an Example...

Property journalist Jenny Knight reflects on 25 years of retirement housing.

'Retirement developments of the past were all too often poky flats with an alarm call system and maybe a visiting warden. Some of the worst had no lifts, no wheelchair access, plugs at floor level and tiny bathrooms and kitchens.

Then there were scandals about service charges which seemed to rise according to the whim of the management company, not according to any established formula. Small wonder that most elderly people chose to stay in their family home for as long as possible.

Then along came English Courtyard with the philosophy that a retirement home should be as elegant and spacious as any other home but also designed and equipped to make life easier for people who might have trouble bending or stretching.

English Courtyard pioneered a new standard of luxury in the retirement sector. The founders' belief was that rooms should be spacious enough for buyers to be able to bring their existing furniture instead of having to shop for half-size tables and sofas.

They introduced handsome cottages and flats which don't look as if they are dwellings for the disabled, but are in fact carefully thought out to help residents cope if their health declines. And they employed a wheelchair bound assessor to check on all the properties to make certain they were suitable for people who might cease to be able bodied.

Thanks to this example, the whole field of retirement dwellings improved massively. On-site staff, communal lounges, activity rooms, guest suites and decent sized grounds became commonplace. The market diversified with some developers aiming at the active retired, building tennis courts and swimming pools and others planning for the older buyer and people who have a second home abroad. Security was improved to appeal to these second homeowners, so they can feel truly confident about locking up and leaving their retirement home.

Bathrooms became both better adapted for the disabled and also more luxurious. English Courtyard introduced the concept of a house which could be converted for downstairs living if necessary, with a wheelchair access shower on the ground floor and a room which could be turned into a downstairs bedroom. From the start English Courtyard set a high standard of design with attractive courtyard schemes looking something like ancient university buildings or 19th century almshouses. The emphasis was on handsome, easy to care for homes with good-looking gardens so that residents could enjoy a delightful green outlook without the labour of the upkeep.

With general improvement in the standard of retirement housing, more people were attracted to the idea of downsizing from their family homes, abandoning maintenance worries and moving into an entirely private cottage or flat where they could find company and support if required. Only one problem remained – people who had lived in substantial houses wanted more space.

On some developments buyers asked for adjacent flats to be knocked through to make a bigger unit. Builders responded by increasing the size of homes. Now retirement developments often offer a range of cottages and flats, giving a choice of one, two or even three bedrooms, a dining room, kitchen, sitting room and sometimes a study or hobbies room too.

Chapter XIV

From Early Retirement Onwards

Mrs Rosemary Wray, the last surviving member of the original residents lived at Manor Court, Pewsey, for 32 years, having arrived in 1980.

Interviewed in 2009 she said:

In October 1980 I saw in the Times Personal column an advertisement saying that there was a flat at Manor Court for sale. I had read about Manor Court a year before. I rang my sister in law in Great Bedwyn and she saw it and said it was just what I needed. I came to see it and the sale was organised in three weeks! I moved in on December 12th 1980.

In a few days I met everyone at a Christmas lunch at the Close Restaurant, now a private house, just over the bridge from Manor Court. Today our residents are still permitted to walk through their grounds, on the way to the village. It was like going to a new school. All were older than me and many were different from my family background of Royal Navy and Royal Marines, but they were all so kind and friendly.

I knew this area anyway because, during the war, my father was in the Admiralty in Bath and we lived nearby and Pewsey, Marlborough, Salisbury and Devizes were all within easy reach.

I have lived at Manor Court since I was 55. Now, nearly 30 enjoyable years later, I really have seen life 'from early retirement onwards' with the English Courtyard Association. Sadly, I am the last of the original residents, though some others have moved on into nursing homes.

Did you make good friends here?
Yes. Of course there were some residents that I scarcely saw, but I made many good friends. There were lots of nice people at Manor Court.

You say there were people from a wide range of backgrounds. How would you describe them?
The residents at Manor Court came from a variety of backgrounds, which made it more interesting. Many came from the professions, what in my day would have been called 'the professional classes', or had been in business. Whenever new residents arrived I always invited them over for a drink.

Did the lifestyle at Manor Court suit you from the start?

Yes, but you needed to involve or develop interests outside life at Manor Court – otherwise there would not have been enough to do!

What were you able to do and to enjoy then?
Obviously I travelled widely, involved myself in charity work, went up to London by train (the train service at Pewsey has always been so convenient for day trips), visited exhibitions and the theatre, as well as involving myself in village activities. I took painting and embroidery courses, attended Marlborough Summer School, and for years I had generations of Siamese cats, usually two of them at a time. Being able to have pets was very important. I also took great pleasure in having my own small garden.

Does life at Manor Court still suit you?
Yes, perfectly: could not be better.

Does it offer you what you need as you get older?
Obviously the ageing process limits you in the things you can still do. Fortunately I have not had a day in bed since I came here. I am a very independent person – but now my sight is bad. I keep my car, but have a former taxi driver from the village drive me as and when necessary. Friends sometimes do my shopping and I have paid cleaning help, and I know the Courtyard Managers will help me in an emergency, but I have always tried not to bother them unnecessarily.

How has your life changed over the last 28 years?
As I said, my sight is bad. I also have MS. My last Siamese cat died recently, and now I will not replace him. Many of my earlier friends are no longer here but I have made new ones – and being on the Courtyard I can see them whenever I want. I can no longer do my garden, but I employ someone to look after it for me. But I would never consider moving to a nursing home. Should ever it be necessary I will arrange nursing care at home here.

What changes would you have liked?
I think it would have been useful if there had been some communal room/area for meetings, entertaining friends and family etc. I know you have a cricket pavilion at Dunchurch that has kitchen facilities. That sounds ideal.

Being the first development you only built 20 garages for 24 properties. I know you now provide all properties with garages – but I was one of the unlucky ones and am rather dependent on friends that no longer have cars letting me use theirs.

The minibus, which you provide at many of your developments, could also have been useful at Manor Court.
What was the average age of the Residents when you first came to Manor Court?

I know, but only because you told me! It was 64, and it does not surprise me. I think part of the reason for this comparatively young age is that the word 'sheltered housing' did not exist when Manor Court was built. No one felt they were moving into an institution. Unfortunately that description gives entirely the wrong impression of what life at Manor Court is like. It is about a life of independence and security that can suit anyone from early retirement on.

Would you recommend people to come to an English Courtyard development?
Yes – perhaps my son-in-law will live here!

At 55?
Certainly, but as I said earlier they would need to travel: create a life outside Manor Court.

At 85?
Of course. I had a friend that did not come to Manor Court until she was well over 90! But you do need to be in good health both mentally and physically.

What do you think are the most important advantages of living at Manor Court?
I can go away and leave my property in safety, thanks to the security provided by Courtyard Managers living on site. My children live only two hours away and my sister-in-law used to live in Great Bedwyn. It is important, when moving to a new area, that you have friends or family nearby. One's grand-children, when they were younger, could come and visit and – as long as they did not cause a nuisance – play in the large grounds. I have also been extremely glad of the guest room and continue to use it frequently. I suppose, to me, the two most important things were the security that Manor Court offered, and the knowledge that my children did not have to worry about me.

Has the support of the Courtyard Managers been a factor in your being able to continue to live here?
The fact that they are there – and available in an emergency – is extremely important. However, I have been fortunate in not having had to call on them for that. They also do a very good job in maintaining the grounds and our properties, but they also do so many small things which make such a difference to our lives here.

One last word of advice?
Come sooner rather than later. Too many people leave it too late. Most residents I know only wish they had come here earlier.

Manor Court, Pewsey

Reproduction of the original architectural drawing by Paul Gibson

Chapter XV

The Courtyards

The English Courtyard Association owns 37 courtyards across 21 counties and has 38 under management including Les Blancs Bois, Guernsey.

1.	Manor Court	Pewsey	Wiltshire
2.	Berrow Court	Upton-on-Severn	Worcestershire
3.	Crittles Court	Wadhurst	East Sussex
4.	Walpole Court	Puddletown	Dorset
5.	Lyefield Court	Emmer Green	Berkshire
6.	Hasells Court	Long Melford	Suffolk
7.	Atwater Court	Lenham	Kent
8.	The Vinery	Torquay	Devon
9.	Hildesley Court	East Ilsley	Berkshire
10.	Malthouse Court	Towcester	Northamptonshire
11.	Hayes End Manor	South Petherton	Somerset
12.	Fullands Court	Taunton	Somerset
13.	Ashcombe Court	Ilminster	Somerset
14.	Framers Court	Lane End	Buckinghamshire
15.	Earls Manor Court	Winterbourne Earls	Wiltshire
16.	Penstones Court	Stanford-in-the-Vale	Oxfordshire
17.	Church Place	Ickenham	Middlesex
18.	North Mill Place	Halstead	Essex
19.	Mytchett Heath	Mytchett	Surrey
20.	Flacca Court	Tattenhall	Cheshire
21.	Dunchurch Hall	Dunchurch	Warwickshire
22.	Bluecoat Pond	Christ's Hospital	West Sussex
23.	Churchfield Place	Girton	Cambridgeshire
24.	St. Luke's Court	Marlborough	Wiltshire
25.	St. Peter's Close	Goodworth Clatford	Hampshire
26.	Northfield Court	Aldeburgh	Suffolk
27.	Timbermill Court	Fordingbridge	Hampshire
28.	Muskerry Court	Rusthall	Kent
29.	Abbey Mill	Prestbury	Cheshire
30.	Sandbourne Court	Bournemouth	Dorset
31.	Turnpike Court	Ardingly	West Sussex
32.	Wyke Mark	Winchester	Hampshire
33.	Eylesden Court	Bearsted	Kent
34.	St. Mary's Court	Beaconsfield	Buckinghamshire
35.	Stuart Court	Minchinhampton	Gloucestershire
36.	Carysfort Close	Elton	Cambridgeshire
37.	Les Blancs Bois	Castel	Guernsey
38.	Motcombe Grange*	Motcombe	Dorset

* Under Management

74

Courtyard Locations

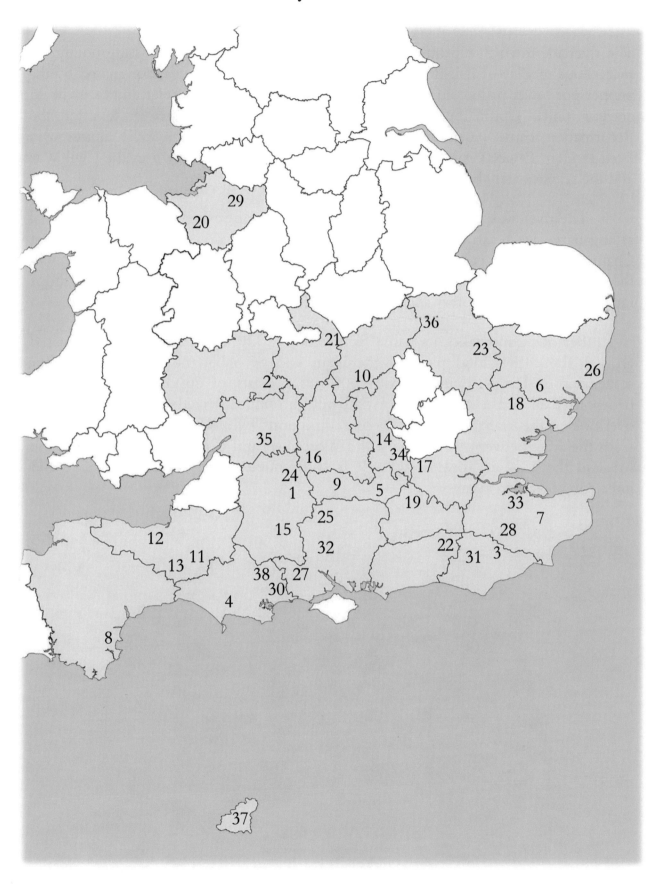

2. Berrow Court, 1980
Gardens Walk, Upton-upon-Severn, Worcestershire WR8 0JP

The riverside town of Upton-upon-Severn, situated at an ancient crossing point, is a marvellous medley of half-timbered and mellowed brick buildings, dominated by the pepper-pot tower of the old church and the soaring spire of St. Peter and St. Paul. In ancient times Upton belonged to the Bishops of Worcester and, after the Reformation, came under the sway of the Bromleys and Martins, local squires who lived at Ham Court. Cromwell's forces attacked and took the town in the Civil War and the scars can still be seen on the old church tower.

The river was once the scene of a busy traffic of Severn trows, the traditional sailing barges that carried goods right up the river and down as far as the Bristol Channel Ports. Now colourful fleets of pleasure craft ply their trade from the quay in the centre of the town and from the new marina. Upton has a wide range of shops including an excellent library and doctor's surgery all within easy walking distance.

Berrow Court takes its name from the area known as Buryfields, the raised ground above the flood plain of the Ham and probably the site of an ancient settlement or Burgh (Berrow). Berrow Court consists of 26 cottages, three two-bedroom flats and a one-bedroom flat, built around a secluded garden courtyard overlooking the Ham. It has good communications by road, being less than a mile from the A38, between Tewkesbury and Worcester, and close to the junction of the M5 and the M50 to Ross on Wye. It is surrounded by beautiful countryside and interesting places to visit.

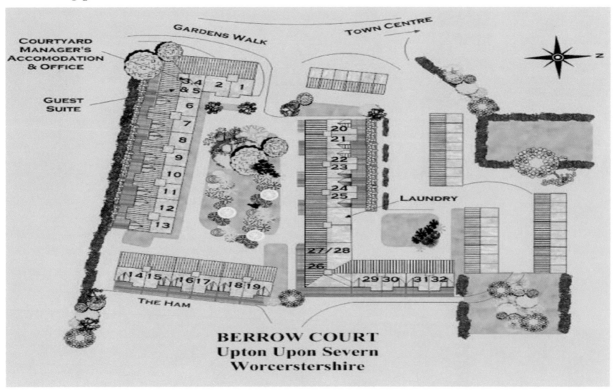

BERROW COURT
Upton Upon Severn
Worcerstershire

Berrow Court

3. Crittles Court, 1981
Townlands Road, Wadhurst, East Sussex TN5 6BY

The hill-top village and former market town of Wadhurst is surrounded by the rolling countryside and woods of the Kent and Sussex Weald. It probably derives its name from Wada, the name of the Saxon tribe that occupied the area and began clearing the forests in the seventh and eighth centuries. Henry III granted the town its charter in 1253. This allowed the town to hold a market each Saturday and a fair on the feast of Saint Peter and Saint Paul, on 29 June each year. Wadhurst's busy High Street offers an excellent array of shops for everyday needs and includes two banks, a post office and a doctors' surgery.

Wadhurst is surrounded by attractive villages and good restaurants. Places of beauty and interest include the Bewl reservoir and Scotney Castle, whilst Royal Tunbridge Wells is only seven miles away. For the commuter, London is 45 miles by car, and one hour and ten minutes to Charing Cross from Wadhurst station. Trains go every hour.

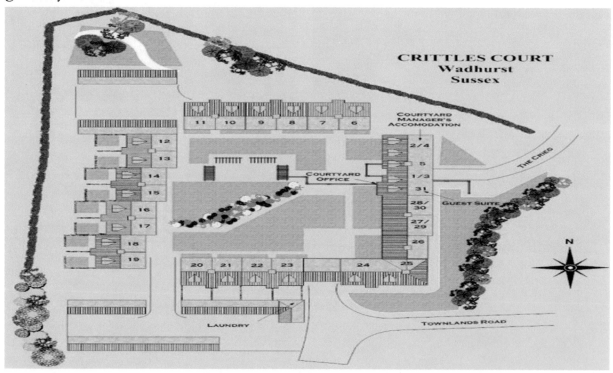

Crittles Court is a delightful development of 30 properties: 17 two-bedroom and – for the first time – four large three-bedroom cottages, and eight two-bedroom flats built in warm brick and tile, with tile-hung facades, traditional to the area. A private walkway connects the development to the High Street. Apart from winning the National Housing Award presented by the National House Building Council, the Royal Institute of British Architects and the Department of the Environment, this development was also commended by HRH Prince Charles in his book A Vision of Britain.

78

4. Walpole Court, 1983
Walpole Court, Orford Street, Puddletown, Dorset DT2 8TH

The delightful and peaceful village of Puddletown, on the banks of the river Piddle, lies in the shadow of the beautiful late mediaeval church of St. Mary, with its seventeenth-century boxed pews, gallery and pulpit. Formerly a market town – the 'Weatherbury' of Thomas Hardy's West Country novels, and where his grandfather once lived – its name was allegedly changed to Puddletown to avoid causing offence to Queen Victoria when she visited the area. Much of the village centre was tastefully renovated at the turn of the twentieth century by the Brymer family, which has added to its charm. Puddletown has enough basic shops for everyday needs, whilst the Roman town of Dorchester, with its wealth of history, culture and shops, lies five miles to the south west. The seaside at Weymouth is just nine miles away. Puddletown is on the A35 Dorchester to Bournemouth road. There are buses to Dorchester, Poole and Bournemouth and an hourly train service from Dorchester to London (2½ hours).

Walpole Court has a total of 24 properties, combining the best of the old and the new. The buildings surround two courtyards, the former stables, garden cottages and walled garden of the beautiful seventeenth-century Islington House, home to the first Lord Walpole (later Earl of Orford), recently superbly restored and still a magnificent private residence. The stables have been converted into four very attractive two- and three-bedroom houses, including the Coach House, whilst the garden cottages have been converted into four spacious two-bedroom flats,

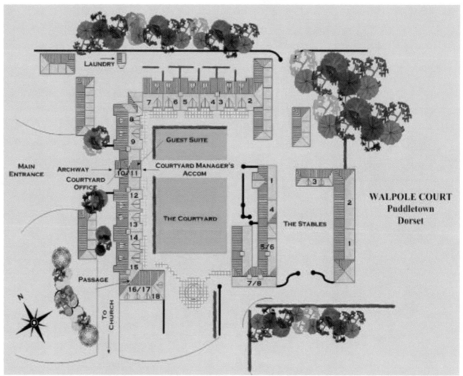

including the bell tower. These are approached from The Square through the black gates of the Islington House drive. The second courtyard consists of 16 new two- and three-bedroom cottages and two flats. These are reached, via Mill Street and Orford Street, through an impressive archway over which are the Courtyard Manager's accommodation and a comfortable guest suite for residents' guests.

Walpole Court

5. Lyefield Court, 1983
Kidmore End Road, Emmer Green, Berkshire RG4 8AP

Emmer Green probably derives its name from the Anglo-Saxon word eamere, meaning a lake beside a stream. A collection of Roman coins, bracelets and pottery found in the area suggests Romano-British occupation from AD 40 until the fourth century. The hamlet, always a small community until the post-war expansion of Reading, was largely dependent for its employment on nearby Caversham Park, an estate listed in the Doomsday Book as being owned by the first Earl of Pembroke, a relation of William the Conqueror. In later years Caversham Park House played host to Queen Elizabeth I, held King Charles I prisoner prior to his execution, and played a vital role in World War II as a BBC monitoring station.

Lyefield Court, built on the former site of St Benet's Home for 'waifs and strays', is now a quiet garden courtyard of 14 two- and three-bedroom cottages and 16 two-bedroom flats a mile north of the Thames. It incorporates a new and impressive flat design: two buildings containing eight apartments on two floors, in the shape of a cross. Their entrance hall and grand staircase are each covered by a domed cupola. Lyefield Court also included for the first time a four- bedroom house at the request of the purchasers.

Secluded from the main road, it borders on Reading golf course and a public open space and is very close to a good small shopping centre, which includes a post office and a bank. Buses go every 20 minutes to Caversham (six minutes) and Reading (20 minutes). There are fast and frequent train services from Reading to London and the West Country.

In 2011 a second phase of nine larger properties (not shown on this plan) was added. Full information on phase 2 is included on pages 156/7.

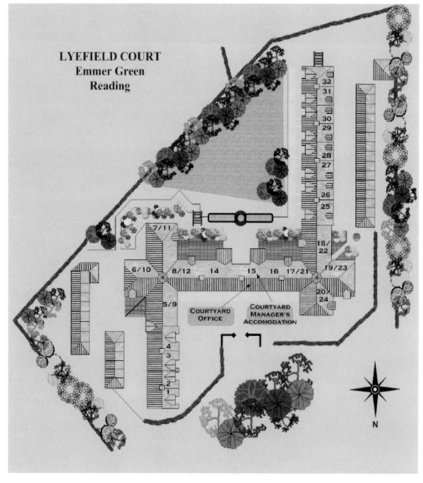

Lyefield Court

6. Hasells Courtyard, 1984
Westgate Street, Long Melford, Suffolk CO10 9DR

Long Melford is a pretty Suffolk village with a long high street and thatched houses, surrounded by glorious countryside made immortal by Constable. Famous for the Church of the Holy Trinity with its fifteenth-century Lady Chapel, its sixteenth-century almshouses and the remarkable Tudor Melford Hall, the village has a full range of shops, good restaurants, post office, library and banks. In more recent times it has become a centre of the antiques trade. During the fifteenth century, the market town prospered from the wool trade.

Frequent buses run to Sudbury (four miles) and Bury St. Edmunds (ten miles) and trains run to London from Sudbury via Marks Tey (1½ hours).

Hasells Courtyard, an exclusive development of nine cottages on the road to Clare, was built on the site of a former coal yard! It was designed to be a pilot scheme to allow the Association to benefit from the use of smaller sites, as these were more easily obtainable: a decision which ECA decided not to pursue on the grounds of economic viability. This, the smallest of ECA's schemes, constructed in the traditional style of Suffolk villages, with finely detailed brick and rendered elevations and pantiled roofs, consists of eight two-bedroom and one three-bedroom cottage surrounding a main landscaped courtyard.

Each cottage is on two storeys with a light and comfortable sitting room, dining room, kitchen and cloakroom on the ground floor and two bedrooms and a bathroom on the first floor. There is no guest suite and the Courtyard Manager lives in a small cottage belonging to the Association directly across Westgate Street.

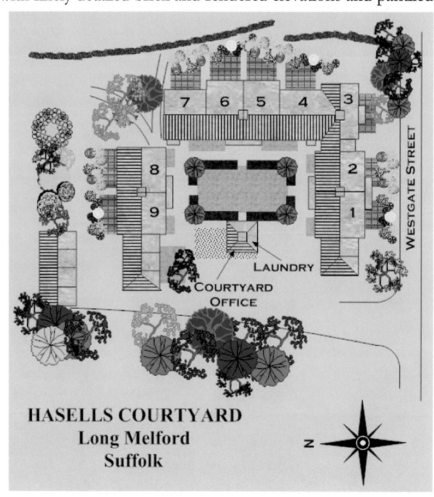

HASELLS COURTYARD
Long Melford
Suffolk

Hasells Courtyard

7. Atwater Court, 1985
Faversham Road, Lenham, Kent ME17 2PW

Lenham is a large and attractive traditional English village with a village square, in the heart of the garden of England, on the southern fringe of the North Downs and half a mile south of the ancient Pilgrims Way. Village life centred round the square; its market and fair dated from the fourteenth and fifteenth centuries. Nearly all the houses date from before 1830. High House and the almshouses on Faversham Road, behind which stands the village gaol, are Jacobean. The village once bustled with activity from trades long since forgotten, as well as its corn market, its stock market in the nearby fields, and visits from the travelling circus. The Dog and Bear, now a hotel with modern facilities, was once a great coaching inn on the old turnpike road from London to Dover. It flourished with the carriage trade, which ended with the coming of the railway.

In the Great War, Lenham was an official staging point for troops on their way to the trenches, whilst in World War II the Battle of Britain was fought in the skies above it, and a US air base was stationed at nearby Egerton. The Lenham White Cross, carved into the chalk on the downs, unveiled on Armistice Day 1922, now commemorates the dead from both World Wars. The village has a wide range of shops to meet everyday needs, including a chemist, post office, banks, library, doctor's surgery, restaurants and a hotel. Served by the M25/M20 and A20 road network, Lenham also has its own railway station on the London-Victoria line. It is 10 miles from Maidstone, and 10 miles from Ashford, the springboard to the continent.

Atwater Court, in the former walled garden and orchard of Grove House, with its beautiful buildings and grounds overlooking St. Mary's Church, provides the courtyard with a perfect setting. Constructed in two separate phases, it now consists of 29 properties: six three- and 15 two-bedroom cottages, and eight two-bedroom apartments surrounding a large lily pond and two court-yards of landscaped grounds.

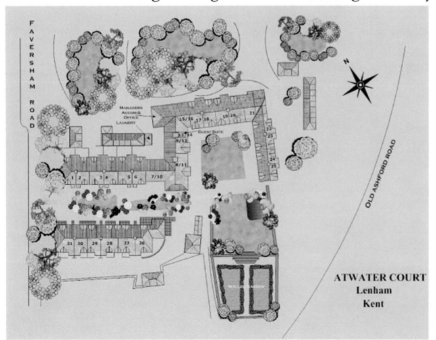

ATWATER COURT
Lenham
Kent

8. The Vinery, 1986
Montpelier Road, Torquay, Devon TQ1 1TY

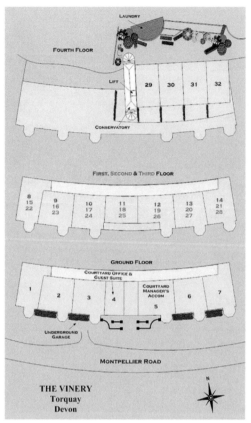

THE VINERY
Torquay
Devon

Torquay, appreciated for its beautiful bay, pleasant climate and sandy beaches, its fine harbour and marina, today is the capital of the English Riviera. The town started to grow after the Napoleonic wars, Tor Bay providing excellent docking facilities for a large naval base, and the families and workers that came with it. With the advent of the railway the town became a fashionable seaside resort for well-to-do Victorians, whose influence on its architecture is still clearly visible. As well as offering excellent shops and a wide range of cultural opportunities, Torquay, the birthplace of Agatha Christie, is surrounded by places of interest. These include Brixham, Dartmouth, Plymouth and a wealth of ancient history and unspoiled country on the moors at Dartmoor. Torquay is easily accessible by road M5/A38/A380 and has fast direct rail services to London (2½ hours from nearby Newton Abbott).

The Vinery, the Association's first town centre development of purpose-built luxury apartments, fully warrants the name 'Courtyard' as it possesses a delightful small garden, formerly part of the gardens of a large cliff-top house, now demolished. This unique feature, together with the conservatory on the fifth floor, offers seclusion and spectacular views overlooking Torbay and the harbour. The Vinery is a magnificent traditional five-storey building, comprising 23 two-bedroom, two three-bedroom, one one-bedroom and four penthouse apartments. All apartments are south facing and, if required, the second bedroom can be converted into a dining room or office, or the wall between the second bedroom and drawing room removed, to provide a larger, double fronted, dining/sitting room.

A classical building embellished by pillars and mouldings, it reflects the origins and style of many of the Victorian buildings in the town. The Vinery is entered through an impressive hallway. A lift is available between the basement garage and the spectacular sunny conservatory on the fifth floor. The Vinery offers wide spacious passages, richly carpeted and ornate entrances to each flat, a comfortable guest suite and resident Courtyard Managers. The Vinery offers the best in secure, elegant serviced living from a former age, whilst providing all the amenities of the town on the doorstep.

9. Hildesley Court, 1986
East Ilsley, Newbury, Berkshire RG20 7LA

East Ilsey, which can be traced back to the Doomsday Book, is a completely unspoilt village nestling in the Berkshire Downs, well known to racegoers as a centre of racehorse training. But from the Middle Ages it was famous as the home of one of England's most important sheep fairs, with flocks of sheep converging on the village across the ancient downland drove roads. Today the sheep are gone and their place is taken by a procession of stately racehorses heading for the gallops on the Downs, and a large colony of ducks whose home is the village pond.

East Ilsey lies just off the A34 Newbury to Oxford road, eight miles north of Newbury and six miles north of Junction 13 on the M4. Oxford is 17 miles away, and Didcot, with regular inter-city trains to London, is 10 miles away. Trains also run from Newbury station. The pleasant market town of Wantage is 15 miles to the east. The village has a regular bus connection with Newbury

Hildesley Court, in the centre of the village, is tucked away across from the duck pond. From the pond a picturesque row of cottages leads to the main entrance archway to the courtyard. The whole development is sheltered in a dip in the hills screened from the north by a belt of large trees. The south facing courtyard is a real sun-trap for all residents to enjoy. For those who love country life it is a delightful place to live.

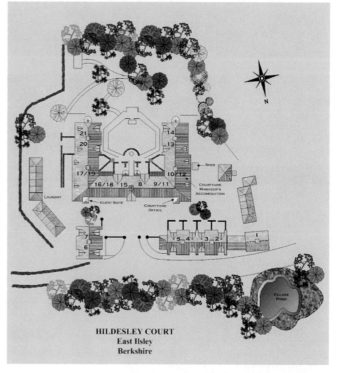

HILDESLEY COURT
East Ilsley
Berkshire

Situated in the lee of the handsome church of St. Mary's, Hildesley Court is surrounded by rolling countryside, pretty villages, pleasant walks and good pubs, two of which are in the village itself. Sadly the village shop and post office recently closed, but both are available in nearby Compton. Residents are also able to the use the internet, which is available in the Courtyard Manager's office, to shop and order on line. Waitrose, Sainsburys and Tesco will deliver to the doorstep. Hildesley Court is a tranquil development of 20 properties overlooking an attractive garden courtyard and pond. There are 13 two- and three-bedroom cottages, some wider, some with conservatories, and seven two-bedroom flats. Upstairs flats have balconies. All cottages and ground floor flats have small private gardens.

10. Malthouse Court, 1988
The Lindens, Towcester, Northamptonshire NN12 6UY

Towcester, the oldest town in Northamptonshire, has a history to match. It dates back at least to the middle of the Stone Age. Evidence exists of Iron Age burials and Neolithic remains. But it rose to importance in Roman times as Lactodorum, a fortified walled garrison town with four gates – two astride Watling Street, the main route to the northwest. In 917, King Alfred's son fortified the town against the Danes and it remained in Saxon hands until confiscated by the Normans under William the Conqueror. In the Middle Ages the town came under the control of a series of Lords of the Manor, the most hated of whom was Richard Empson, tax collector for Henry VII. Happily for the town he ended his days beneath the executioner's axe on Tower Hill. In the Civil War, Towcester was again fortified, and Prince Rupert stationed his ordnance there. On his withdrawal the Parliamentary army camped there on their way to defeat the Royalists at Naseby.

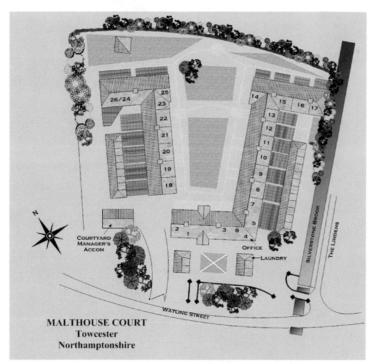

MALTHOUSE COURT
Towcester
Northamptonshire

But it was the age of the stage coach that brought elegance and wealth to Towcester in the eighteenth and nineteenth centuries. Watling Street by then had become the main route to Holyhead and Dublin, along which countless travellers, Swift and Dickens among them, passed this way and stayed a night or changed their horses at the Saracen's Head or the Talbot Inn (now Sponne House).

Today, Towcester is a thriving market town with a wide range of shops and other facilities, as well as a popular racecourse. It is served by a comprehensive road network – the A5 to Milton Keynes (12 miles), the M40/A43 from London and the A43/M1 to the north. The nearest train stations are at Northampton and Milton Keynes.

On entering Malthouse Court through an impressive stone archway, the bustle of Watling Street gives way to an oasis of peace and tranquillity. 26 two- and three-bedroom cottages and apartments, built in the traditional South Northamptonshire style, surround a grassed courtyard beyond which lies the parkland of Easton Neston. Towcester's market place and many shops are less than 100 yards from the entrance.

Malthouse Court

11. Hayes End Manor, 1989
Hayes End, South Petherton, Somerset TA13 5BE

South Petherton is a beautiful Somerset village with a history stretching way beyond the Dark Ages. The Fosse Way and the ancient British track that is now the A303 both pass through the parish. The name comes from the river Parrett, which flows northwards towards the Bristol Channel. South Petherton has all the amenities of a small town with a bank, library, doctor's surgery, post office and a good range of shops all gathered under the shadow of the beautiful octagonal church tower, a short walk from Hayes End. Towns and villages in this part of Somerset are blessed with lovely honey-coloured Ham stone, which is still quarried from nearby Ham Hill. The tradition of working in this stone is very much alive and a great deal of the mason's craft has gone into the restorations and new buildings at Hayes End. South Petherton lies just to the north of the A303, six miles east of Ilminster and seven miles west of Ilchester. Yeovil is 11 miles away and Taunton and the M5 motorway 16 miles.

Hayes End Manor is a fine example of an ancient Somerset farmhouse, dating perhaps from the fourteenth century. Many historic features have survived from the early days when it was a timber framed open-hall house. The present development, part of a long process of change, is based on the old farmhouse with its pretty secluded courtyard and its beautiful stone flax barn and granary, all listed buildings. A further 11 cottages have been built to

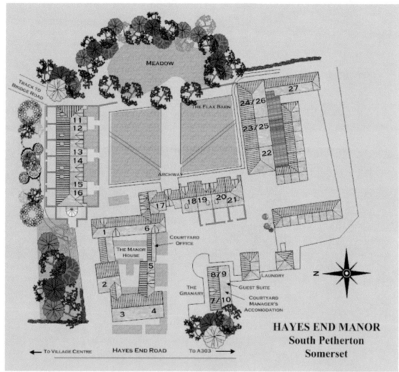

form a second larger courtyard round the former farmyard and the flax barn and granary have been turned into flats and maisonettes. The Manor Farmhouse buildings have been carefully restored to make six lovely houses with some very interesting features. Much care and skill has gone into creating houses and flats to the highest modern standards of comfort and insulation.

The extensive well-maintained grounds are spectacular, as well as providing the opportunity for keen gardeners to have additional allotments and the use of a greenhouse.

12. Fullands Court, 1989
Shoreditch Road, Taunton, Somerset TA1 3YF

The county town of Taunton, on the river Tone, has a history stretching back to Saxon times. It is the rural and cultural centre of Somerset, an area surrounded by beautiful country, abounding with historic houses and places of interest and on the edge of Exmoor and the Quantocks. Taunton County Cricket Ground, the racecourse, golf courses, the Brewhouse Theatre and the Castle all add to the variety of life it offers, as do its excellent communications The M5 exit gives easy access to the Midlands and the South West, whilst the inter-city train service to London, Paddington takes 1¾ hours; Bristol is an hour and Exeter 30 minutes.

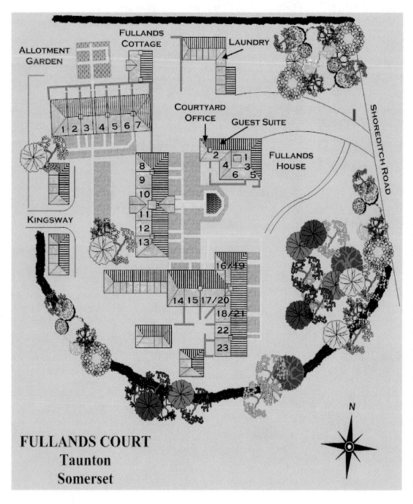

FULLANDS COURT
Taunton
Somerset

Fullands House, which has been completely restored, is a fine late Georgian building and the centre piece of Fullands Court. It has changed ownership and its use many times over the years, at different times housing military commanders, friars, lunatics and then – for much of its later life – schoolboys, amongst whom was General Gordon of Khartoum. From 1946 it was part of Kings College. Fullands was also closely associated with the formation of the Somerset County Cricket Club, hosting the first matches ever played there by the county.

Fullands Court consists of 30 houses and apartments surrounding two contrasting courtyards. Fullands House has been converted into three two-bedroom apartments and three one-bedroom apartments. Fullands Cottage, a pretty Victorian cottage with its own garden, has also been converted - and 17 new two- and three-bedroom houses, and six new two-bedroom flats complementing the architecture of Fullands House, have been built in the grounds. A frequent shuttle bus service to the town centre stops at the gates.

13. Ashcombe Court, 1990
Ashcombe Lane, Ilminster, Somerset TA19 0ED

Ilminster – 'the Minster on the River Ile' – is a busy Somerset town built of mellow honey-coloured stone from Ham Hill. Minster denotes a Saxon religious centre known to have flourished here in the eighth century. But the splendid perpendicular church, the glory of the town – and one of the grandest and loveliest parish churches in England – dates from the fifteenth century. The Square with its pillared market building is a few minutes' walk from Ashcombe Court, and the town has all the shops and amenities one could wish for, almost on the doorstep.

Ashcombe Court is built in the grounds of Summerlands House, a fine listed building dating from the 1830s. The house and the Malthouse – also a listed building – are incorporated in the development, and form an interesting contrast to each other and to the new buildings. Summerlands House is approached from the central courtyard by an imposing flight of steps.

The new buildings of Ashcombe Court consist of a central and southern courtyard, contrasting and complementing each other. The central courtyard is entered by an archway, through a finely proportioned pedimented building of Ham stone with stone pilasters surmounted by a cupola, giving access to seven new cottages and eight new flats, as well as to Summerlands House. The southern courtyard of eleven new cottages, built in stone, is approached from Ashcombe Lane. In total, the development comprises thirty-one fine properties.

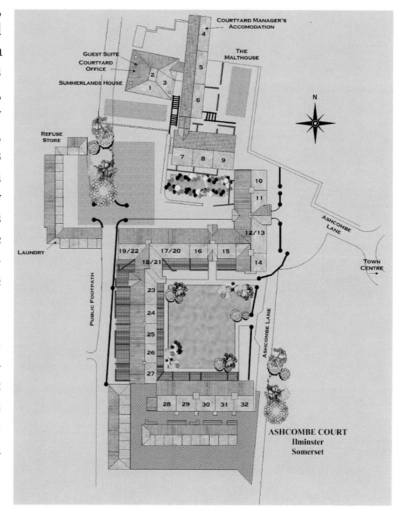

Ilminster lies on the A303 13 miles west of Ilchester: a by-pass takes the through traffic well away from the town. It is 14 miles from Yeovil and Taunton and 12 miles from the M5 motorway.

14. Framers Court, 1991
Ellis Way, Lane End, Buckinghamshire HP14 3LL

Lane End is a pretty village of mellow brick and flint buildings and duck ponds high in the Chilterns close to Marlow, High Wycombe and Henley. The village possesses excellent village shops, a bank, post office, hairdresser, doctor's surgery and a fine selection of pubs. Marlow, on the banks of the Thames, is only four miles away with all the shops and facilities of a fashionable English country town.

Lane End dates from Victorian times; its principle industry was chair-making and the local craft 'bodgering'. The bodger chopped timbers, cut them into rough legs and turned them on a primitive lathe. The chair legs were sent to the workshop where they were assembled by the framer. The finished chairs were then packed and conveyed by horse and wagon to London. At this time chairs were being produced at a rate of 4,700 a day. The iron foundry and agriculture provided most of the other local jobs. Local wheat and barley supplied the breweries of Marlow and Henley.

Framers Court is a development of 27 properties, just off the High Street, tucked into a sheltered hollow. It consists of two courtyards of cottages, maisonettes and apartments, and the name commemorates a small Victorian chair-makers' workshop that stood on part of the land. The entrance is flanked by three flint and brick cottages and an archway leads to the lower courtyard of eight more cottages and four sunny ground floor apartments. A grand flight of steps leads to a more formal courtyard of six cottages and six very spacious maisonettes. A further flight of steps leads through another archway and a lychgate to Framers Alley and the village centre. All levels are accessible without the need to climb stairs. Mellow and red brick and flint contrasts with grey brick panels echoing the most striking features of the old village houses.

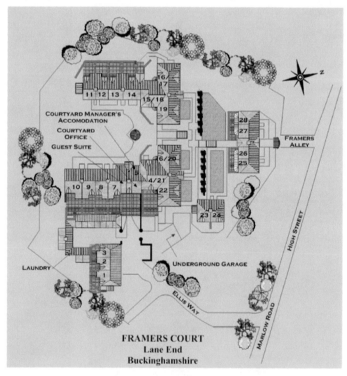

FRAMERS COURT
Lane End
Buckinghamshire

Lane End lies on the B482 just south of the M40. It is four miles from Marlow, six miles from the centre of High Wycombe and eight miles from Henley. The M4 at Maidenhead (Junction 8/9) is nine miles away. London is 45 miles and Oxford 24 miles.

15. Earls Manor Court, 1992
Winterbourne Earls, Salisbury, Wiltshire SP4 6EJ

Nine hundred years ago William the Conqueror granted Winterbourne Earls to William Longespee, Earl of Salisbury. Today, with its sister villages of Winterbourne Dauntsey and Winterbourne Gunner, it is surrounded by green fields through which the River Bourne flows. Old Sarum is nearby, and the Roman road from Winchester to the Mendips passes below the village. The Winterbournes share a well-stocked shop and post office, a handsome Victorian church and a new church hall, all within a few minutes' walk of Earls Manor Court. Stonehenge, Woodhenge and the iron-age hill forts of the Figsbury Ring are close by, and bear witness to this being one of the earliest inhabited areas of England, whilst Salisbury, with its beautiful Cathedral and Close, offers wonderful cultural opportunities and good shops, and is just three miles away.

Earls Manor Court is a magnificent development of 20 two- and three-bedroom cottages and apartments set in the former farmyard of the beautiful seventeenth-century manor house, which it adjoins. It is built in brick, flint and a chequerboard of flint and stone that is a feature of many old buildings on the Salisbury Plain. The fine Chilmark stone, from the same quarry used to build Salisbury Cathedral, is superbly set off by knapped flint, warm red brick and tiles.

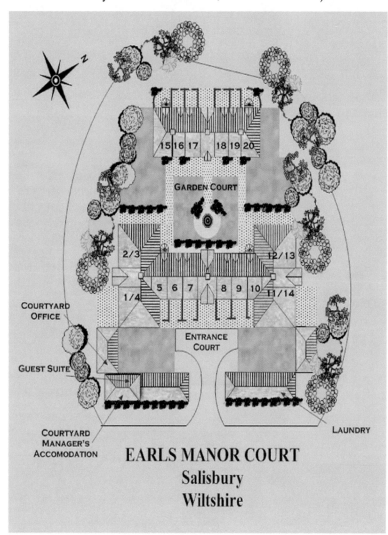

EARLS MANOR COURT
Salisbury
Wiltshire

Upon entering the courtyard – and passing through the archway – time stops still. Peace and tranquillity reign in the small but exquisite garden. Surrounding the Courtyard are eight two-bedroom cottages, eight two-bedroom apartments and four three-bedroom cottages, the additional room of which is over the archways, providing an ideal study or third bedroom.

16. Penstones Court, 1993
Marlborough Lane, Stanford-in-the-Vale, Oxfordshire SN7 8SW

Stanford-in-the-Vale lies between Farringdon and Wantage on the A417 (six miles distant from both). The rail networks of Oxford and Swindon are 30 minutes' drive. Surrounded by Iron Age hill forts, overlooked by the White Horse at Uffington and the ancient Ridgeway track connecting the Marlborough Downs to the Chiltern Hills, Stanford-in-the-Vale takes its name from Saxon times, an ancient stony ford crossing the river Ock where today the bridge spans the river. Founded as early as 939, the medieval glory of this rural village is the church of St. Denys on the green. Largely undisturbed until the Civil War, legend has it that the village almost certainly hosted Cromwell in his failed attempts to capture the royalist stronghold of nearby Farringdon House. Shortly after, in 1646, the village suffered an attack of the plague which took the lives of 33 local people in under three months. The opening of a turnpike road between Wantage and Farringdon, the opening of the Wiltshire and Berkshire canal (now closed), and the opening of a Great Western Railway station at nearby Challow led to an expansion of the village. But this slowed in the mid-nineteenth century following the agricultural depression.

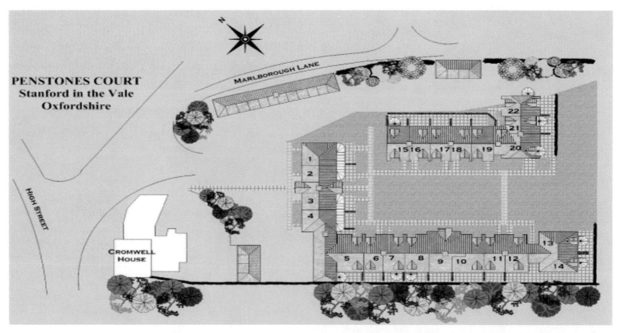

Penstones Court is built in the former farmyard of Penstones Farm, now Cromwell House. The Cotswold stone of the buildings, taken from the Swell quarry, and the clay tile roofs mould into the village as if they had been there for centuries. The Courtyard, open to the south, consists of a variety of 22 delightful two- and three- bedroom cottages, some with additional features, including sun rooms and conservatories. The extensive grounds include an attractive garden, a meadow, pond and unbroken views over the Vale of the White Horse. There is also an excellent allotment area for keen gardeners, and a minibus to take residents on shopping and other trips.

Penstones Court

17. Church Place, 1994
Austins Lane, Ickenham, Middlesex UB10 8XB

Ickenham, until the arrival of the railway in the early 1900s, was a remote rural village, 16 miles west of London, dominated by the church and its glebe land, the three country estates at Swakeleys House, Ickenham Hall and Buntings, and farmland. For centuries the principle employment in the area was domestic and agricultural. At the time the population was little more than 300 people. The only access to the capital was by muddy village roads through Pinner and Harrow or Hillingdon village and Ealing.

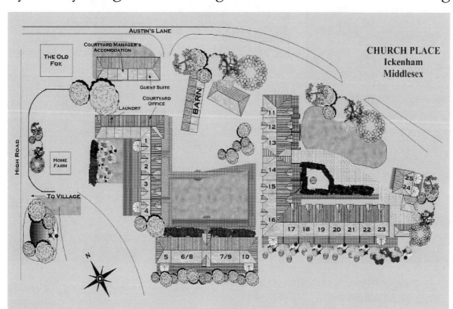

The opening of a railway station, Ickenham Halt, in 1905 and the extension of its platform in 1922, allowing it to cope with more than three carriages at a time, changed everything. The railway brought with it a developers' boom. The large estates and farmland were transformed into housing estates. The formation of the Royal Flying Corps, the forerunner of the Royal Air Force, resulted in the construction on farmland at Ruislip, Ickenham and Northolt, of Northolt Aerodrome. The ornate village pump and pond, the church of St Giles dating back to the fourteenth century, the road names, the Coach and Horses Inn, all remain links with Ickenham's past. Today, Ickenham is a thriving bustling London suburb, with a wide range of shops and other facilities, served by the Metropolitan and Piccadilly lines. This makes it a Mecca for commuters and a paradise for local pensioners, who may use its rail service to London free of charge!

Church Place, built in the former paddock and farmyard of Home Farm, where cattle still grazed and grain was stored in its barn until 1992, is an extremely popular English Courtyard Association development. It enjoys easy access to central London and, via the M25, easy access to Denham and the surrounding countryside. 21 spacious two- and three-bedroom cottages, some with conservatories, all with private gardens and garages, and four large two-bedroom apartments, surround two beautifully landscaped courtyards. The first – dominated by the magnificently restored barn, now listed and used for residents' social events and hobbies – connects, through an archway, to the second, laid out in a more formal style.

18. North Mill Place, 1995
Mill Chase, Halstead, Essex CO9 2FA

Halstead, a quintessential East Anglian country town on the Essex/Suffolk border, takes its name from the Saxon words meaning a healthy place to live. The Saxons established themselves and the market (originally sited in the middle of the town) by the sixth century, long before the Norman Conquest. The Grammar School dates back to 1594. Initially a small rural town, its growth was much affected by the Industrial Revolution and the advent of the railway. Samuel Courtauld's silk weaving mill, in the old town watermill, was built in 1827. This changed life in the town dramatically and it became, in time, the largest employer of labour, predominantly women, in the area. The iron foundry, flour mill, brewery and wood turning were other local industries. Halstead's two impressive churches, Saint Andrew's and Holy Trinity, stand guard at either end of the town, which has all the amenities required for everyday needs, including a small cottage hospital to the rear of North Mill Place. The Roman town of Colchester (12 miles), Braintree (7 miles), and Sudbury (10 miles) and a fast train service from Chelmsford (19 miles) to London are all within easy reach.

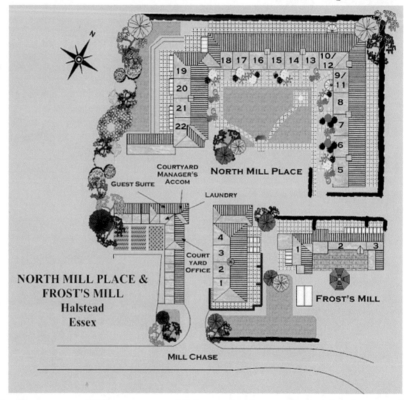

Frost's Mill, on Mill Chase, is the former home and family business of the Frost family who owned the Mill since 1720 and provided corn and animal feed throughout North Essex, until it closed in 1989 after over 250 years. Although the sails and tower of the windmill have been removed, the machinery has been preserved and its buildings extended and converted into three delightful and unique two- and three- bedroom dwellings facing the 'stump' in the old mill yard, whilst their gardens front on to the courtyard.

North Mill Place, built in the former paddock of Frost's Mill, complements its architectural style and consists of 14 spacious new two- and three-bedroom cottages and four large apartments. These surround three sides of a delightful courtyard, in the middle of which are a magnificent walnut tree and a pond.

19. Mytchett Heath, 1995
Mytchett Place Road, Mytchett, Surrey GU16 6DP

The village of Mytchett in Surrey, close to Camberley, the Royal Military Academy at Sandhurst, Pirbright and Bisley, has always had strong connections with the British army. Many of its road names commemorate events connected with the Boer War. Mytchett itself has limited shopping facilities, but Camberley and the busy market town of Farnham are within easy distance by car, and Mytchett Heath has its own minibus, operated by the Courtyard Managers,

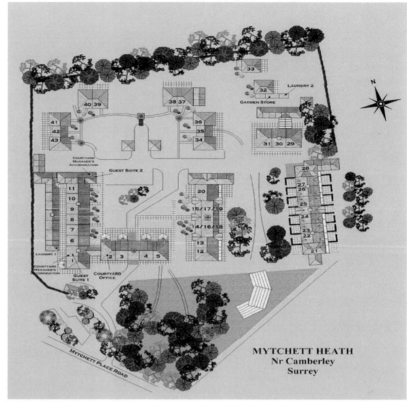

MYTCHETT HEATH
Nr Camberley
Surrey

which is available for shopping trips and other outings. Fast trains from Woking to London and easy access to the M3 to London and the South West make it a very convenient place to live.

Mytchett Heath, surrounded by woods and heathland, is on the recently restored Basingstoke Canal. It adjoins the Canal Centre, which celebrates the history of the canal and is a good place for tea on a warm summer day. Mytchett Heath is the Association's largest development in England (Les Blancs Bois in Guernsey is the largest). Constructed in two phases, it consists of 43 houses and apartments and introduces for the first time the wing house, in response to purchasers' requests for larger properties. The grounds, formerly the site of a school, were once the preserve of a former head gardener with a passion for unusual and exotic trees. Mytchett Heath now benefits from the fruit of his work, the results of which can be seen today. The centrepiece of the first phase is an impressive three-storey building of spacious luxury apartments, on either side of which is a courtyard of delightful two- and three-bedroom cottages built in different styles in red brick with blue headers with red tiled roofs. Variations include some double garages. Phase II consists of a courtyard of six large wing houses – those on the east and west side are separated by a standard two-bedroom cottage. Two detached wing houses and three two-bedroom cottages effectively complete the eastern courtyard of Phase I. The wing house is described in detail in the chapter on Properties.

20. Flacca Court, 1996
Field Lane, Tattenhall, Chester, Cheshire CH3 9PW

Tattenhall is a pretty rural farming village eight miles southeast of the beautiful Roman town and cultural centre of Chester. Although it is thought that a church existed on the site at the time of the Norman Conquest, St. Alban's church in the centre of the village dates from the early sixteenth century. But it was the building of the Chester Canal in 1770 (now the Shropshire Union Canal) that ultimately began to bring prosperity to the area, firstly by providing work on the canal's construction and, on its completion, by the transportation of cheese and dairy products to other parts of the country. The railway followed, with lines to Chester and Crewe and later to Whitchurch. Until it closed, Tattenhall station was of local importance and resulted in the creation of a number of substantial Victorian houses in the area. Tattenhall is a thriving village offering good shops, including a post office, butcher, grocer, chemist and surgery, as well as a variety of cultural and sporting opportunities, and is a very friendly place to live. The M53 to Liverpool and M55 to Manchester are within easy reach, whilst the gateway to Wales and the Snowdonia National Park is eight miles away at Wrexham. There is also an excellent rail network at Crewe.

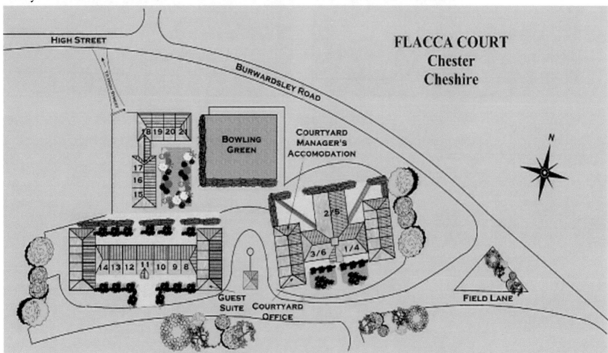

Flacca Court is a delightful development of 14 elegant two- and three-bedroom houses, with a variety of conservatories and sunrooms, and six spacious two-bedroom flats. Upstairs flats have balconies and those downstairs have sun rooms. The Courtyard is enhanced by its traditional English setting, accentuated by beautiful views overlooking the cricket pitch and beyond to the Peckforton Hills. Flacca Court has its own minibus, which is available to take residents shopping to Chester or on other trips, and the use of an excellent bowling green, which is part of the development. The cricket pavilion opposite the Courtyard hosts many Flacca Court social events.

21. Dunchurch Hall, 1997
Southam Road, Dunchurch, Rugby, Warwickshire CV22 6PD

Dunchurch is a delightful and historic village, complete with stocks, maypole and village green, and many old half-timbered and thatched sixteenth, seventeenth and eighteenth-century houses, set in the beautiful Warwickshire countryside. The village has a wide range of shops and services, as well as an excellent hotel/pub, the Dun Cow, on the Coventry/Daventry and Southam/Rugby crossroads. Dunchurch became famous – or infamous – through its role in the Gunpowder Plot. Sir Everard Digby, Robert Catesby and their fellow conspirators stayed at the Red Lion, now Guy Fawkes House, to await news of their plan to blow up the Houses of Parliament. For centuries Dunchurch was a popular stopover in the days of the stagecoach; up to 40 coaches a day used to stop and take on fresh horses whilst their passengers refreshed themselves. The infamous highwayman Dick Turpin was based there for many years. Today Dunchurch offers easy access to Rugby (three miles), the M45, M1, M6 and M40. Inter-city and local rail services are available in Rugby.

Originally built as a hunting lodge for the Duke of Buccleuch in 1840, the Hall became Dunchurch Hall School in 1883, amalgamated with Winton House School in 1940: it closed in 1993. The site was acquired for the Association for a development of 23 properties and opened in 1997. The Hall has been converted into three magnificent apartments, a Manager's office and a guest suite; the original stable block was converted into two cottages, and 18 new two- and three-bedroom cottages and flats were built in the grounds. In 2006 a second phase of five additional properties were built: four wing houses and a traditional cottage.

The magnificent grounds overlooking the ha-ha, were recently extended by some five acres to include a pond, wild flower garden and meadow and a number of other improvements, thanks to the great generosity of two of our residents. The development also boasts a former cricket pavilion, now converted and much used by residents for a wide range of communal activities, and a minibus and CCTV.

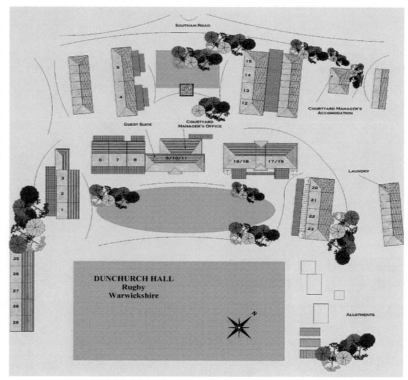

22. Bluecoat Pond, 1997
Christ's Hospital, Horsham, West Sussex RH13 0NW

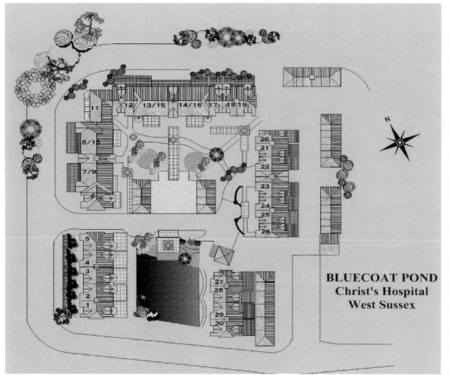

BLUECOAT POND
Christ's Hospital
West Sussex

Christ's Hospital has its roots in Newgate in the City of London. In 1552, encouraged by a sermon by the Bishop of London, Nicholas Ridley (later one of the Oxford martyrs burnt at the stake), Edward VI founded Christ's Hospital. Since its formation the School has been heavily endowed by the Livery Companies and continues to honour the Founder's wish to select and support a high proportion of disadvantaged children. In 1897 the foundation stone was laid for a new school at a site near Horsham and in 1902 pupils moved from London to their new site. In 1985 the girls were reunited with the boys when they moved to Horsham from Hertford. Its magnificent chapel, Globe-style theatre, Olympic- size swimming pool and Sports Centre may all on occasion be enjoyed by ECA's residents. On school days the renowned Christ's Hospital band may be seen playing the students in to lunch. Christ's Hospital has its own railway station: trains go to London, Victoria and good road links exist via the A24. A wealth of shops and cultural pursuits are also available in the pleasant nearby market town of Horsham.

Bluecoat Pond, situated on the former Christ's Hospital dairy site, takes its name from the long blue coats still worn today by the students. The Victorian pond and water tower are the centrepiece of this spectacular courtyard of 36 spacious properties and the beautifully landscaped grounds. These include a first phase of 22 two- and three- bedroom cottages and eight two- and three-bedroom flats in the main court-yard, and a second phase to the south (added in Autumn 2004 but not shown on the map) of four wing houses and two two-bedroom cottages, built on the west side of the road dividing the two. Residents also benefit from the availability of two comfortable guest suites, where friends and family may come to stay, and our own minibus which is available to take residents on shopping and other trips.

116

23. Churchfield Court, 1998
High Street, Girton, Cambridgeshire CB3 0XA

Girton combines the advantages of country living with the grace, beauty, culture, shops and academic lifestyle of Cambridge. The history and life of Girton have centred round St. Andrew's Church and Girton College. Both have had a huge influence and impact on English social behaviour and thinking. The original church of St. Andrew, founded in Saxon times, has remained virtually unchanged for the past 500 years. During the Middle Ages, Girton Guilds were formed. They organized welfare for the poorer members of the community and maintained a form of insurance for its members, the elderly and widows.

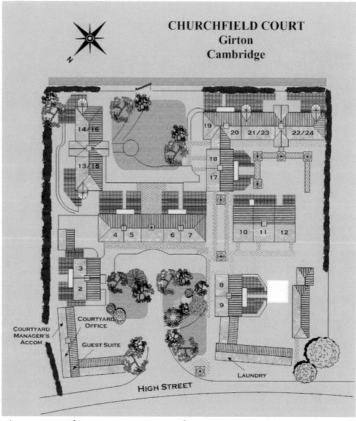

The Guilds were craft-based, bringing together master craftsmen, journeymen and apprentices from many different trades. Girton College, which takes its name from the village, was established in 1873 for the education of women, by Barbara Bodichon and Emily Davies. Emily Davies wrote in her pamphlet Women in the Universities of England and Scotland, 'the aim of these colleges will not be directed to changing the acceptance of women, but rather to securing that whatever they do shall be done well... their work suffers from want of training'.

The village offers a village store and post office, two pubs, a tennis club and a golf course, whilst Histon, a few minutes distant, provides a wide variety of shops and services as an alternative to driving into Cambridge. Girton village is off the A1307 Huntingdon Road and close to the A14. Churchfield Court is at the north end of the High Street, past St. Andrew's Church, on the fringe of the village, in a former farmyard. It consists of 23 properties surrounding four courtyards with extensive views over the meadow and the fields beyond. Properties include 15 attractive two- and three-bedroom cottages, many of which have conservatories, and eight spacious two-bedroom apartments. Churchfield Court has attractive well-maintained grounds and a popular allotment area as well as several acres of meadow, often important for those with pets. There is also the Association's own minibus, which is available to take residents on regular shopping trips to Cambridge or trips to other areas.

Churchfield Place

24. St Luke's Court, 1999
Hyde Lane, Marlborough, Wiltshire SN8 1YU

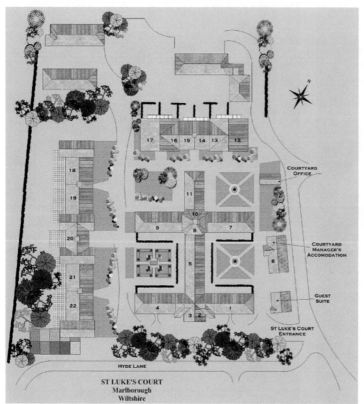

ST LUKE'S COURT
Marlborough
Wiltshire

The historic town of Marlborough is well provided with shops, including Waitrose, and restaurants, tearooms and essential services alongside its fine wide, largely Georgian, High Street. Two churches stand in elevated positions at either end of the town, whilst to the west is Marlborough College, the famous boarding school, which dates from 1843. Together town and gown offer many cultural opportunities. The town first appeared in the Doomsday Book and received its Royal Charter from King John in 1204. Cardinal Wolsey was ordained in St. Mary's church in 1498. The town supported Parliament in the Civil War and was sacked by the Royalists; scars of the battle still remain. To the east lies the Savernake Forest, established by William the Conqueror as a Royal hunting ground; it covers some 2,300 acres, one of the largest and oldest forests in England, and offers wonderful walks and glorious scenery. Henry VIII, who wooed Jane Seymour in the Forest, was the last monarch to use it.

St. Luke's Court, which overlooks the Common and the Marlborough Downs, is an extremely impressive and successful Courtyard, sympathetically combining the best of the new with the old. It includes a magnificent conversion of the former stone Workhouse, built in 1837, which contains five two-bedroom houses, five two-bedroom apartments, and a maisonette overlooking the whole Courtyard. Six new two-bedroom cottages have been added, which match the architecture of the Workhouse. In addition, five new houses – four of them large wing houses with integral garages, in the Victorian style of the former matron's house (since demolished) complete the interesting, varied and spacious array of 22 properties. Following the cruciform of the original Workhouse, there are four charming individual gardens, each with a different theme. These were once the exercise yards separating men from women, and boys from girls – who were never allowed to meet or socialise. St Luke's Court is nine miles west of Hungerford on the A4 and 11 miles from Junction 14 on the M4. Fast trains go to London and the west from Pewsey, which is eight miles away. The Courtyard also has its own minibus.

25. St Peter's Close, 1999
Church Lane, Goodworth Clatford, Nr Andover, Hampshire SP11 7SF

Goodworth Clatford, 'the ford where the burdock grows', straddles the river Anton, a tributary of the Test. It is a peaceful small English village in a rural setting, with a church, two pubs, village store and post office. Just one mile to the south is the busy town of Andover, whose services meet all day-to-day needs. Its location makes this a perfect home for country lovers and fishermen! Goodworth Clatford is at the head of the beautiful Test Valley. Country lanes wend their way south beside the River Test, through Longstock, the market town of Stockbridge with its attractive shops and good restaurants and the headquarters of the exclusive Houghton Fishing Club, Kings Somborne, and on to the ancient and historic town of Romsey with its magnificent Abbey, the cultural centre of the valley. Not only does the Test provide some of the best fly fishing in the world, in the past its many mills provided the livelihoods of those living there. The weaving of cloth and the milling of grain brought prosperity and sustenance to the whole area, halted only by the devastation caused by the Black Death. Later, brewing and tanning became important industries.

St. Peter's Close, lying beneath the shadow of the bell tower and octagonal spire of St. Peter's church, is a picturesque development built on two levels in traditional brick and flint, with views over rolling countryside. The centrepiece is a fine listed timber-framed barn, which spans the entrance to the main courtyard of 19 properties: 15 two-bedroom cottages, two three-bedroom and two two-bedroom apartments, set in beautiful landscaped, well-maintained grounds. St. Peter's Close also has its own minibus available for shopping trips to Andover and other areas. Goodworth Clatford is just off the A303 to Basingstoke, where it joins the M3 to London. Fast trains run from Andover to London, Waterloo. Stockbridge is five miles away and Romsey 12 miles.

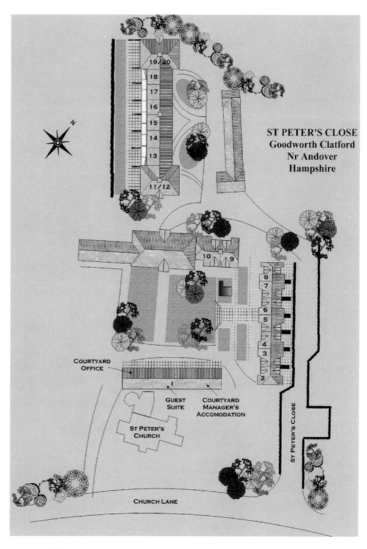

ST PETER'S CLOSE
Goodworth Clatford
Nr Andover
Hampshire

26. Northfield Court, 2000
St Peter's Road, Aldeburgh, Suffolk IP15 5LU

Aldeburgh's story is the story of the Suffolk coastline and its battle with the sea. By 1500 the town, despite losing six streets to the sea, was emerging as a port and its prosperity grew. Fishing and boat building are still prominent features of the town and

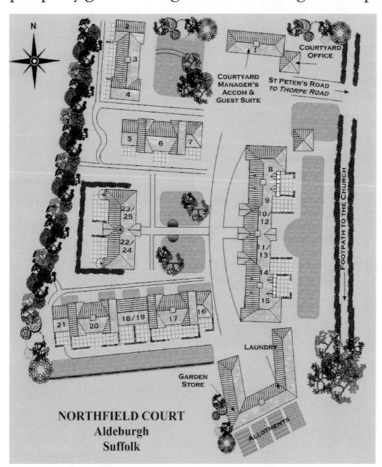

both trades still thrive. Fishing huts and boats lie on the pebbled beach, just as they have for years. In spring and winter, when the tourists are gone, it is as if time has stood still. Aldeburgh is surrounded by places of interest. The Martello Tower and Moot Hall (now a museum) in the town, the coastal forests of Tangham, Tunstall and Dunwich (once the second largest port in England until devoured by storms), the Norman castles at Framlingham and Orford, romantic Leiston Abbey, the Blything Union Workhouse chapel at Bulcamp, and the bird sanctuary at Minsmere are all monuments of national, local and natural history.

This delightful, unspoilt seaside town has a wide selection of restaurants shops, galleries, inns and hotels, as well as a good golf course and a small cinema. Every year the town hosts the world- renowned Aldeburgh Festival founded by the composer Benjamin Britten and tenor Peter Pears: it is also the setting for George Crabbe's poem The Borough, now better known as Britten's opera Peter Grimes.

Northfield Court lies at the end of a short quiet road, beyond which are open fields. It is a short walk to the sea and town centre. A tree-lined path leads to the beautiful parish church of St. Peter and St. Paul. The development also has its own minibus, which is available for shopping and other trips. This delightful Courtyard offers a variety of 24 spacious properties, including 10 two- and three-bedroom cottages, eight two-bedroom apartments and six wing houses, set in attractive well-maintained private grounds. London is approximately 100 miles by car. Trains from Saxmundham (6 miles) go to London, Liverpool Street (two hours).

Northfield Court

27. Timbermill Court, 2000
Church Street, Fordingbridge, Hampshire SP6 1BB

Fordingbridge, an attractive historic market town with an impressive seven-arched bridge that elegantly spans the River Avon, is the northern gateway to the New Forest. The town was formerly the home of Augustus John. From earliest times the area was inhabited, as evidenced by the Neolithic and Bronze Age artefacts that are still to be found. The Roman villa at Rockbourne is nearby, as is the beautiful Saxon church at Braemore, whilst St. Mary's Church dates back to Norman times, and the late-Victorian Union Workhouse – built to house 100 inmates – reminds us of the harsher realities of the agricultural and industrial revolution. Much local history is connected with the New Forest, and the fight of commoners to keep their rights. William the Conqueror requisitioned the Forest as a royal hunting preserve, imposing draconian penalties on those that failed to obey the law. Later the Crown's requirements for timber to build ships for the Navy also caused controversy. Not until the mid-nineteenth century were the rights of commoners fully recognized. Today the New Forest is a centre for horses and riding, where wild ponies and cattle control the roads and are left in peace to graze!

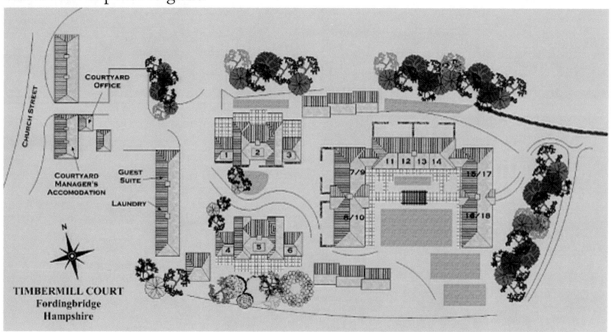

Timbermill Court, approached by the A338, is seven miles south of Salisbury and 12 miles north of Bournemouth. It is a secluded development of 18 properties, set in beautiful landscaped grounds off Church Street, beside the water meadows of the River Avon and in the shade of St. Mary's Church. The Courtyard, of 20 properties in brick and flint, consists of four wing houses, six two-bedroom cottages, three three-bedroom flats and five two-bedroom flats. It also has its own minibus which is available for shopping and other trips. The bustling High Street, with a wide range of shops, banks and other facilities, including the town hall, library and community centre, is just a short walk away.

28. Muskerry Court, 2001
Nellington Road, Rusthall, Tunbridge Wells, Kent TN4 8SX

The village of Rusthall on the A264 is only a mile from the spa town of Tunbridge Wells, 10 miles from East Grinstead and 3½ miles from the A21. The first record of Rusthall dates from the eighth century, when Egeburth, the Anglo-Saxon king of Kent, granted the lands to the Bishop of Rochester. It predates by several centuries the existence of its more famous neighbour, Tunbridge Wells. Rusthall may have been so named because the local water becomes rust-coloured from the iron in the rocks. It too had its own tourist attractions, attracting visitors to Toad Rock, which resembles a sitting toad on an outcrop of sandstone, and to its 'cold bath'. Pelton's 1881 Guide to Tunbridge Wells describes Rusthall as 'a pleasure garden, laid out by James Long, the owner, in 1708, around a cold bath fed by springs'. A series of pools descended to the valley below and a lengthy rock-hewn staircase led down from Rusthall Common to the boathouse. By 1818 the gardens were revived as tea gardens. In 1895 a house (now the Beacon Hotel) and the gardens were developed as private grounds. Today touches of Rusthall's former grandeur remain, whilst the village provides good basic facilities to meet everyday needs.

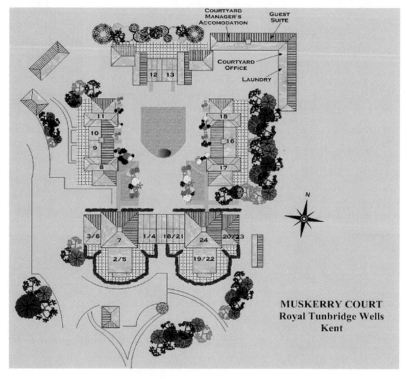

MUSKERRY COURT
Royal Tunbridge Wells
Kent

Muskerry Court, in a classical English parkland setting, was inspired by the architecture of Decimus Burton, who was responsible for building Calverley Park in Tunbridge Wells and the Palm and Temperate Houses at Kew. It takes its name from Lord Muskerry, who acquired the Manor of Rusthall in 1664. Muskerry Court is situated in beautiful mature grounds. It is a magnificent development of 23 spacious properties comprising six wing houses, three cottages (No. 16 has a third bedroom and a third reception room) and 14 two-bedroom apartments, two with roof gardens. It is approached down a tree-lined drive – which it shares with Rusthall Lodge, a private nursing home, which has recently been extended and modernised – through an impressive archway leading into the courtyard. Muskerry Court has its own minibus which is available to take residents on shopping and other trips. There is also a community medical centre at the drive entrance.

Muskerry Court

29. Abbey Mill, 2002
Shirleys Drive, Prestbury, Cheshire SK10 4XY

Prestbury, on the Cheshire/Lancashire borders, two miles north of Macclesfield and 14 miles south of the centre of Manchester, is an oasis. Commuters travel to work in the neighbouring towns, whilst others enjoy their retirement in this attractive thriving village in the centre of dairy farming country. The Jacobean and Tudor estates of Aldington Manor, Gowerworth Hall, Capesthorne Hall and Prestbury Hall remind us of the wealth of our architectural and historical past that surrounds the village. Prestbury takes its name from early Saxon times, meaning a fortified priests' town. St. Peter's Church, one of the oldest parish churches in the country, with religious roots dating back to 653 AD, was restored by Sir George Gilbert Scott in the late nineteenth century. A Norman chapel, its predecessor, can be found in the churchyard.

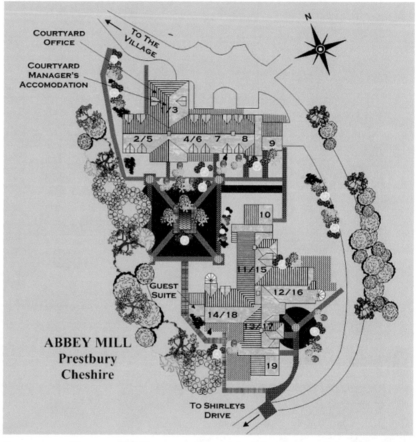

Prestbury Mill, fed by a millstream branched from the River Bollin, was grinding corn over 700 years ago. By the end of the eighteenth century the mill had become a cotton factory, before changing once more to meet the fashionable requirements of the silk trade. It closed at the end of the nineteenth century, before finally being demolished in 1964.

Abbey Mill, a superb development of 18 properties which adjoins St. Peter's Church, is built in red brick with blue headers and a grey tile roof. The northern half of the development may be accessed from an entrance beside the church and the southern half from Shirleys Drive. Abbey Mill, built on the site of the old corn mill overlooking the River Bollin, consists of 13 spacious apartments and five houses, with under-ground parking. Prestbury village, with its excellent amenities including a good variety of restaurants, is a short walk away. It also boasts its own train station and a golf club. It is within easy reach of Manchester International airport and the Peak District National Park. Stockport and the M63 are six miles to the north.

130

30. Sandbourne Court, 2002
54 West Overcliff Drive, Bournemouth, Dorset BH4 8AB

Bournemouth, with its miles of sandy beaches, mild climate, and some of the driest and warmest weather in England, is a desirable place to retire. A wealth of beautiful coastline also provides a fascinating geological and fossil record of Jurassic Britain. Situated at the mouth of the river Bourne, on the former hunting estate Stourfield Chase, it is hard to believe that in 1800 it was largely barren heathland, frequented only by a few fishermen, turf cutters and smugglers. It developed in Victorian times as a destination for affluent holidaymakers and invalids seeking the sea air. Its growth and prosperity were much influenced by Dr Greville's Spas of England and the arrival of the railway. Today Bournemouth and the adjoining towns of Poole and Christchurch form the regional centre of business, education and culture in the south west. Bournemouth University provides the town with a youthful as well as traditional image and Bournemouth's International Centre, Symphony Orchestra and Arts Institute have brought business and cultural regeneration. The commercial and civic centre is the Square, from which the gardens descend to the seafront and the pier. Shopping streets are mainly pedestrianized and offer a vast choice of modern shopping malls, major stores and Victorian arcades. Bournemouth has excellent communication links: by rail to London, Waterloo; by road to the M3/M27 network; and by air from Bournemouth International Airport.

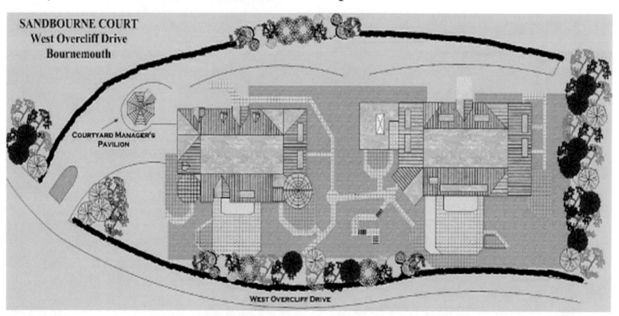

Sandbourne Court, set in attractive landscaped grounds, is a new development of 16 luxury two-bedroom apartments, built in elegant Edwardian style in two separate buildings, in the fashionable conservation area of Alum Chine. All apartments have south facing patios, balconies or roof terraces and each has its own car space in the secure underground garage beneath the buildings. There are lifts from the garage to all floors. The sea front and the tropical gardens are a short walk away, as are the shops and amenities of Westbourne Village. The Courtyard also has its own minibus.

Sandbourne Court

31. Turnpike Court, 2003
Hett Close, Ardingly, West Sussex RH17 6GQ

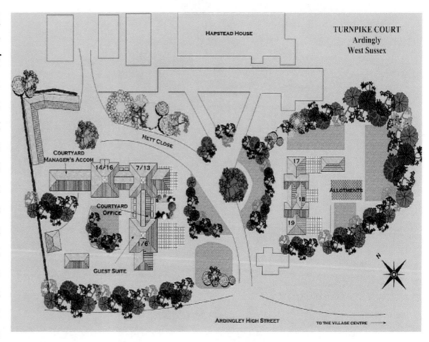

Ardingly is a delightful village surrounded by woods in an area of Outstanding Natural Beauty. It has good basic shops, including a post office and a bakery, and is 3½ miles from Haywards Heath and six miles from East Grinstead. The village dates from Saxon times, when a forest clearing was created on high ground near a tributary of the River Ouse which runs across this part of the Weald. Later the Normans founded a church, replaced in the mid-fourteenth century when the village had become wealthier through the wool trade by St. Peter's Church. Ardingly has many other attractions of note, including the South of England Agricultural Society Showground which hosts many country events, the South of England Horse Trials, the Spring Garden and Leisure Show, the Autumn Show and Game Fair, and the Ardingly International Antiques and Collectors Fair. Ardingly Reservoir, which offers the opportunity to sail and fish, is nearby, as are Wakehurst Place, the country branch of the Royal Botanic Gardens at Kew, and Ardingly College, an independent well-established Woodard co-educational school for boarders and day pupils aged 3-19. The original railway to the village closed in 1963, but the track was acquired by the Bluebell Line, whose long-term aim is to extend it to Ardingly.

Turnpike Court is situated in the grounds of Hapstead House, a Victorian mansion now converted into flats and approached from the High Street and Hett Close. Turnpike Court is an impressive development; the front doors open into a magnificent entrance hall which leads to the lift and 16 luxurious two-bedroom apartments on three floors overlooking an attractive private garden and Hapstead House. On the east side of Hett Close are two spacious 2/3-bedroom wing houses and a two-bedroom house, surrounded by beautifully maintained gardens and lawns.

Residents have the use of their own minibus service, which is available for shopping and other trips. Haywards Heath has an excellent fast train service and Gatwick airport is a twenty-minute drive.

32. Wyke Mark, 2003
Dean Lane, Winchester, Hampshire SO22 5DJ

The walk through water meadows, from the lovely Hospital of St. Cross (England's oldest alms-houses, built in 1136 and still lived in today), past the cricket ground, to Winchester College and the magnificent Cathedral, shows off Winchester's full majesty and glory, and has remained virtually unaltered for 600 years.

Several times in its history Winchester fell victim to pestilence and war. The Black Death allegedly wiped out half its population in 1348, returning again in 1361 and spasmodically reappearing for several centuries thereafter. The town paid a price in two civil wars. Empress Matilda besieged Winchester Castle in 1135 and imprisoned King Stephen before herself being besieged by forces raised by King Stephen's wife. Cromwell occupied Winchester in 1645, destroying the Castle, of which only the Great Hall remains. Peace and culture returned to Winchester in Georgian times, when many houses were built, or restored with Georgian façades, but it was not until the arrival of the railway in 1840 that prosperity returned.

Wyke Mark is a development of 25 luxurious, spacious two-bedroom apartments surrounding a horseshoe-shaped courtyard off Dean Lane, set in a wooded and airy suburb on the north side of Winchester, only minutes from the town centre. The apartments, in the grounds of a former substantial private house, are built on two and three floors, serviced by lifts. All have views over the garden, and each has a patio, balcony or roof terrace and their own entry 'phone. CCTV oversees the grounds. Local shops, including a bank, chemist, newsagent and supermarket, are only a short walk away at the south end of Deans Lane, on the Stockbridge Road. Residents have the use of their own minibus for shopping and trips further afield, whilst Winchester, which adjoins the M3, has excellent road and rail communications.

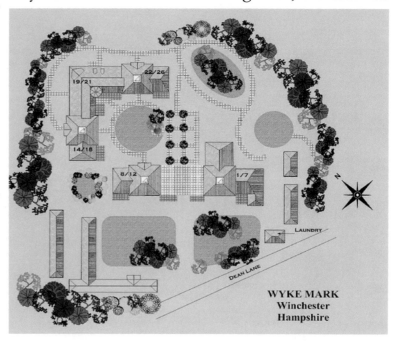

33. Eylesden Court, 2004
The Green, Bearsted, Maidstone, Kent ME14 4BF

The settlement of Bearsted can trace its beginnings to pre-history and it is believed that habitation of sorts began in 4000 BC when farmers moved into the area. Early remains have been found in Hog Hill and Ware Street. Although Holy Cross Church can trace its origins back to before 1066, Bearsted is not mentioned in the Doomsday Book. Bearsted is a quintessentially English village. Two public houses on the green – the White Horse Inn and the Oak on the Green – continue to be the centre of village life; previously they were not only local inns, but local justice was dispensed from both premises. Many famous persons have lived in Bearsted, including the cricketer Alfred Mynn, known as the Lion of Kent, who was one of the first to master overarm bowling. He lived in Ware Street, is buried in Thurnham churchyard, and is featured on the village sign. The village green cricket ground is said to be one of the oldest in Kent.

Eylesden Court, set back from Bearsted's village green, provides 22 beautiful properties including nine wing houses, two three- and seven two-bedroom cottages, and two three- and two two-bedroom apartments, arranged in a courtyard, around their own 'village green' and orchards. Residents enjoy croquet on the lawn in the summer months, as well as the use of additional allotments. The development also benefits from having its own minibus to take residents on shopping and other trips. Bearsted has excellent communications; it is a short distance from Maidstone, just off the M20, and has its own railway station.

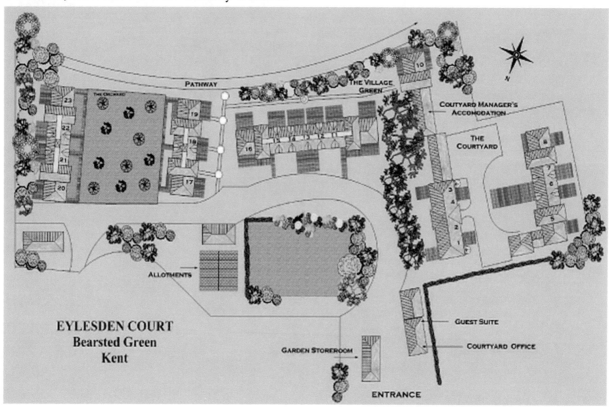

Eylesden Court

34. St Mary's Court, 2005
Malthouse Square, Beaconsfield, Buckinghamshire HP9 2LG

Beaconsfield is a busy market town, 25 miles west of London, in the Chiltern Hills. The surrounding countryside is largely arable, but small beech forests still remain. The old town is 'striking from the spaciousness of its street lined thoroughfare containing many good examples of 18th century red brick houses, many being older timber structures refaced' (Buckinghamshire by C.E. Roscoe). It allegedly derives its name, not from the 'field of the beacon' as many suppose, but from 'a clearing among the beeches'. In the days of the stagecoach, Beaconsfield was the first stop on the road from London to Oxford. A number of former coaching inns still remain today. Old Beaconsfield was for many years the constituency of Benjamin Disraeli, who lived at Wycombe and who later took the title of Earl of Beaconsfield. Poet and politician Edmund Waller of Hall Barn (now the home of Lord Burnham), lived there during and after the Civil War. Other residents include Edmund Burke and the author GK Chesterton: all are buried in the churchyard. Beaconsfield New Town, now the commercial centre, one mile north of the Old Town, was established with the arrival of the railway at the end of the twentieth century, and the creation in 1919 by local Quakers of Bekenscot, the first 'model village'. From the mid-seventeenth century there had been a significant Quaker influence in the area; William Russell, one of the first Quakers, used Jordans Farm in Seer Green as a Meeting Place in 1659. William Penn, founder of Pennsylvania, worshipped there regularly. His family are all buried at Seer Green. In recent times a number of films and TV productions have been filmed in the area, due to the closeness of Pinewood Studios.

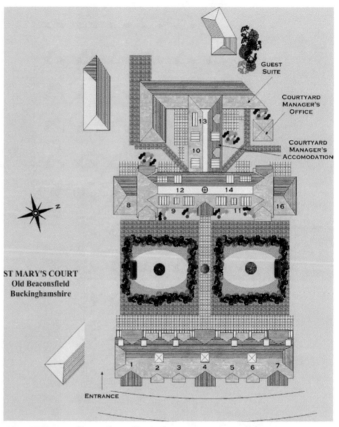

St. Mary's Court comprises 15 spacious properties: two houses, seven cottages and six spacious apartments arranged in two groups on either side of a landscaped courtyard. Properties range between 1100 and 1450 square feet in size, with private patios or balconies. St. Mary's Court is just off the Market Place of the Old Town, with a wealth of facilities – shops, restaurants and church – on its doorstep. It has excellent road and rail communications to London.

St Mary's Court

35. Stuart Court, 2006
Butt Street, Minchinhampton, Stroud, Gloucestershire GL6 9JB

Minchinhampton is one of the Cotswolds' best kept secrets. Largely untouched by modern development and surrounded by common land, the village rises high above the neighbouring towns of Stroud and Nailsworth, looking down on the beautiful valleys below. At its centre stands the columned seventeenth-century Market House, and opposite is the twelfth-century Church of the Holy Trinity. Minchinhampton, in its heyday, was an important town in the area. Built of local stone from nearby quarries to the north of the parish, many of its buildings date from the seventeenth and eighteenth centuries – the great days of the wool trade which gave it its importance. Eight mills of the former Manor are listed in the Doomsday Book. The area is steeped in history, and traces of the Iron Age are clearly visible; a defensive network of bulwarks stretches across the Common for nearly a mile, probably a former settlement of the Belgic Dobunni tribe. Many Neolithic and Bronze Age long and round barrows break the skyline, an archaeologist's paradise! The Common, the alleged site of the Battle of Ethandune where King Alfred defeated the Danes in 879, is an area of some 600 acres of rough pasture, where wild flowers grow and Commoners continue to exercise their rights to graze their horses and cattle. Minchinhampton is an idyllic, thriving Cotswold village with a church, several shops, bank, library, doctor's surgery, post office, three good restaurants and a golf course. It lies ten miles west of Cirencester, five miles north of Tetbury and four miles east of Stroud. The nearest railway station is at Stroud.

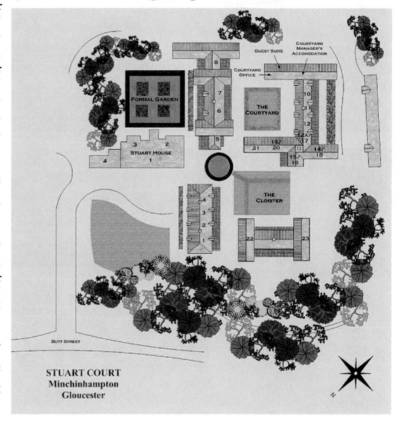

Stuart Court, a delightful development of 26 spacious and attractive properties set in beautiful grounds, has the former rectory, Stuart House, as its centrepiece. The Courtyard includes four wing houses, ten two-bedroom cottages and eight two-bedroom apartments, with Stuart House converted into four further apartments. A private path leads to the centre of the village and its excellent facilities. The Courtyard also has its own minibus service to take residents on shopping or other trips.

36. Carysfort Close, 2007
Overend, Elton, Cambridgeshire PE8 6RW

Elton is a delightful, unspoilt small village, ten minutes' drive from the charming market town of Oundle, famous for its public school. A large part of the village is in

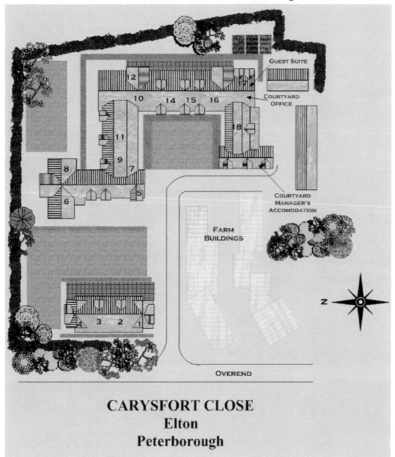

CARYSFORT CLOSE
Elton
Peterborough

the ownership of the Elton estate, 3,800 acres of parkland, farms, houses, cottages and commercial property, the centrepiece of which is Elton Hall and its magnificent gardens, home to the Proby family since 1660. A house has existed on this site from Norman times. Today, what you see is largely Jacobean, but if viewed at a distance from the south it creates a fairyland fantasy of turrets, pinnacles and towers. The Hall houses an impressive art collection and one of the finest private libraries in the country, including an extremely rare Henry VIII prayer book. The village possesses a post office, a small general store, the beautiful thirteenth-century church of All Saints, two pubs and a fish restaurant, as well as the estate garden centre. The Hall gardens are open every weekend. The nearest towns for shopping are Oundle (three miles) and the cathedral city of Peterborough (ten miles) from which trains run frequently to London, Kings Cross in under one hour. Elton is 86 miles north of London via the A1. Exit on the A605, after three miles turn right for Elton.

Carysfort Close is the Association's most recent development. Situated at the upper end of Overend opposite All Saints Church, the properties are largely constructed of locally quarried limestone, which allows the development to blend naturally into its traditional surroundings. The 17 properties – eight cottages and nine flats – are grouped round two formal courtyards in the shadow of the former ironworks, now more of a barn than an iron foundry and housing some of the earliest agricultural machinery made in the agricultural revolution. Residents benefit from their own minibus which is available to take them on shopping trips to Oundle and surrounding areas.

Chapter XVI

Les Blancs Bois, 1985
Rue Cohu, Castel, Guernsey GY5 7SY

Although Guernsey is geographically much closer to France than the UK, its loyalty to the Crown can be traced to Norman times when the Channel Islands first became part of the English realm. It suffered harshly as a result of German occupation in the 1939-45 war. Today the island is self-governing and enjoys the same level of independence as it has since first becoming a part of the United Kingdom. Guernsey's ability to look after its own fiscal affairs has meant that it has been able to foster a favourable tax climate. This has led to offshore banks, fund managers and insurance companies establishing themselves here. However, the traditional industries of flower and tomato growing, fishing and dairy farming still play an important part in contributing to the varied economy and to the island's character. Guernsey's capital city, St Peter Port, has been a busy port since Roman times. The deep, safe anchorage, and relative remoteness from France, made St Peter Port the Channel Islands' premier port, graced by a wealth of ship builders, privateers and merchant adventurers. Georgian and Regency styles enriched the architecture and the culture of the island, as did an influx of French emigrés including Victor Hugo.

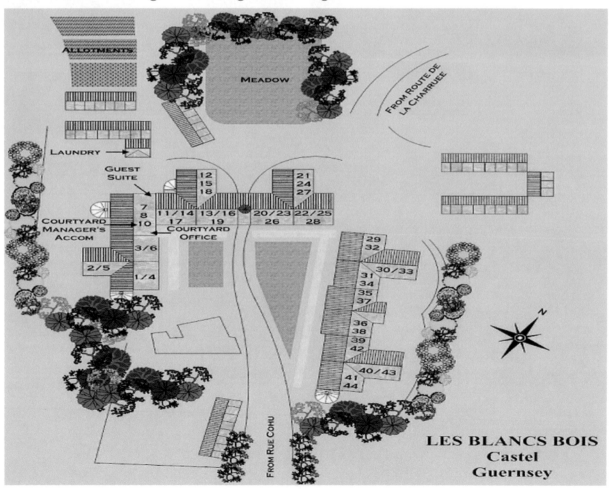

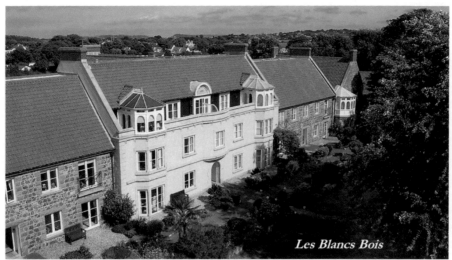

Les Blancs Bois

Les Blancs Bois, in the parish of Castel in the west of the island, is about one mile from beautiful Cobo Bay. Cobo has a convenience store, garage, bank and restaurant. The architecture of Les Blancs Bois is based on the traditional Guernsey farmhouse and local granite has been extensively used in the development to fit into the landscape. The intention to create a collegiate atmosphere of elegant and relaxed proportions, enhanced by the courtyard, gardens and surrounding paddocks, has been admirably achieved. The buildings are principally on two floors, but also include six second-floor apartments and two first-floor maisonettes. Many apartments have conservatories and those on the ground floor have patios. Eleven of the 44 apartments can be occupied by non-domiciled people who have already lived in Guernsey for ten consecutive years or more. The other 33 can only be occupied by Guernsey-born residents. The site's minibus goes to St Peter Port every Tuesday and on alternate Fridays; on Thursdays the minibus goes to one of the island's supermarkets. The heron, the ECA symbol exhibited on the roofs of most ECA developments, was the winning design in a competition held for Guernsey school children.

Photograph:
Christopher Thornhill with John Gummer, Minister of Agriculture, Fisheries and Food - and the heron - at Northfield Court, Aldeburgh.

Chapter XVII

Motcombe Grange, 2010
Motcombe, Shaftesbury, Dorset SP7 9HJ

My first introduction to Motcombe Grange was in the spring of 2006, when two friends from Kenya whom I had known for almost 50 years contacted me. Having returned to England and moved to Motcombe Grange they were now thinking of selling their property and moving closer to family. They wondered if I could help as they were having problems with its sale, so I drove over to see them.

Motcombe Grange was an up-market retirement development, meeting similar needs to the English Courtyard Association but offering more services. In many ways its concept, in terms of style and service, were halfway between those provided by a standard ECA development and the original concept for the Worcestershire Hotel at Droitwich.

The development had been well designed, blending old and new construction very effectively. My friends had an attractive, spacious and bright apartment on the first floor overlooking the grounds. Of particular interest were the additional features offered, including an impressive modern kitchen quite capable of producing meals for 80-plus residents twice a day, a large dining room, drawing room and bar.

On many occasions since the original Worcestershire Hotel idea, ECA had been asked if they would ever consider producing meals, and the decision had always been no. ECA's policy was to provide residents with facilities for them to have meals in their own homes. This gave them a greater degree of independence and reduced the service charge; it also avoided giving a development an 'institutional' feel. But Motcombe Grange did not feel institutional. It had the feel of an English country house hotel.

Motcombe Grange is situated in the small village of Motcombe in Dorset, in the Blackmoor Vale, nine miles from Shaftesbury, on the borders of Wiltshire, Somerset and Dorset, with Bath, Salisbury, Bournemouth and Yeovil all within a 30-mile radius. An impressive brochure offered purchasers *a village shop (and Post Office) two churches, a hotel, two public houses – whilst Port Regis School offers the facilities of Motcombe Park Sports Centre'*. These included a 25 metre swimming pool, sauna, gymnasium, a nine hole golf course, tennis and squash courts. Membership of the Sports Centre was available to the residents of Motcombe Grange.

Motcombe Grange, built as a substantial private house in 1900, became a preparatory school in 1937 and existed as such for 65 years. It closed in 2002 and was bought by the owner of a care home near Gillingham, whose idea was to combine the concept of 'independent living' with a 'menu of care' supplied by the care home.

Motcombe Grange

The brochure also offered:

Motcombe Grange

'a provision of fully managed services, maintenance and emergency call bell facility with the opportunity to purchase additional support and assistance when required from the Menu of Care.'

Within the Grange is a gracious dining room, drawing room, snooker room with bar and library, a gym and hairdressing salon. A croquet lawn is located in the grounds of the Grange.

All ground floor apartments have patio doors leading from the sitting room to the gardens. All first floor apartments have balconies. Most homes have two bedrooms, however there are several offering 3 bedroom accommodation. Live in management offers help and advice and a 24 hour emergency response service'.

In many ways Motcombe Grange had much to recommend it, although sales were going through difficult times and residents and potential purchasers seemed unsure exactly what services were included in their service charge. The two factors combined meant that there was little I could do to help my friends with their sale, but eventually they were able to let their apartment and move nearer to Basingstoke to be closer to their family. These problems and others became much clearer two years later, when Christopher Mackenzie-Beevor, whose home was only five miles from Motcombe village, was approached by someone whose parents lived at Motcombe Grange and who wanted to find out whether the English Courtyard Association would consider taking over the management.

It appeared that concern and dissatisfaction had been growing for some time amongst the residents of Motcombe Grange over how their development was being run. On closer investigation it appeared that the management company and the development were, to all intents and purposes, one and the same organization, and this had led to a conflict of interests.

One of the things that the English Courtyard Association got right from the outset – and it is a lesson worth noting – was the decision to separate building from management. History shows that it is wise to allow the building and financing arm to make a once-and-for-all profit on the sale of their houses and apartments, and for the management and caring arm to remain a non-profit making organization. This is particularly true when building for the retired. There needs to be seen to be total transparency and a clear separation of the two functions and their costs, including keeping separate management accounts which should be regularly available for inspection by residents.

Interior Photographs of Motcombe Grange

Bridge room

Drawing room

Hairdressing Salon

Fitness suite

Kitchen

Dining room

Bar

Billard room

This really did not appear to be the case at Motcombe Grange. The owners appeared to be financing the construction, managing the development and providing the nursing care package. The result was that residents were unclear and confused as to what services they were entitled to from their service charge, and what additional charges were being made. The dividing line of responsibility between the builder, day-to-day management and nursing care appeared clouded.

From the residents' viewpoint it appeared that Motcombe Grange's management were maximizing profit not only on the sale of their properties, but on the services provided as well. Although there may be nothing unlawful about maximizing profit - in a situation where potentially vulnerable residents need care and security, it is understandable if this leads to dissatisfaction and discontentment.

ECA were interested and prepared to consider taking on the management of Motcombe Grange, providing that all the residents wished them to do so and providing that the residents accepted that, over time, their development would be run on ECA lines. The owners were also enthusiastic for ECA to manage Motcombe Grange; they had little desire to continue to manage it in the current circumstances.

A meeting with the residents of Motcombe Grange was arranged on 28 May 2009. It was attended by ECA's managing director Charles Clayton, Christopher Mackenzie Beevor and myself, together with the owners of Motcombe Grange and their solicitor. Having heard exactly what we were able to offer, the residents voted unanimously for the English Courtyard Association to take over the management.

It took a number of months before the final handover was agreed, not least because ECA insisted on owning the freehold of Motcombe Grange once all the properties had been sold, as was our policy with all our own developments. Meanwhile ECA agreed to take over the management of Motcombe Grange with immediate effect, and in due time the freehold.

I was delighted with the outcome and considered the addition of Motcombe Grange to the ECA fold to be of great importance. Motcombe Grange was able to offer proper meals in a proper dining room, and a number of other facilities that are not available at normal ECA developments. Such facilities could well appeal to ECA's own residents, who might be glad to have more services and care as they become older and more frail, whilst still maintaining an independent ECA style of life.

So it was with great pleasure that I learnt that the first resident from an ECA development had moved into Motcombe Grange.

The point had been proved!

Motcombe Grange

Chapter XVIII

Lyefield Court – Phase II, 2011

Lyefield Court's second phase was the last development to be designed specifically for the English Courtyard Association. Designed by Richard Morton, a senior partner in Sidell Gibson whose architectural practice designed all ECA's developments, it adjoins and complements the ground-breaking first phase of 30 properties designed by Giles Downes some 25 years earlier. That first phase achieved national acclaim and did much to influence and shape the aspirations of future generations in the private sector wishing to enjoy an independent life in retirement in comfort and security.

Although the second phase had reached an advanced stage by 2008, work was halted due to the ensuing recession and was not completed until 2011, by Beechcroft Developments, who had previously acquired the site. As the years have gone by, so has the demand for larger properties. It is very appropriate, therefore, that Phase 2 offers some of the largest properties provided by the Association.

The nine spacious new properties include: two three-bedroom wing houses, each with a terrace garden; three two-bedroom ground floor apartments, each with two terraces; and four three-bedroom first floor maisonettes, two of which have an additional dressing room/study, and all of which have at least one balcony on each floor. All maisonettes are approached by a passenger lift from the ground floor entrance hall, and all properties have garages close by. All residents in Phase 2 enjoy the use of the facilities of Phase 1, which include the grounds, guest suite and Courtyard Manager service.

Emmer Green is well stocked for local amenities. It offers a health centre and all the shops necessary for day-to-day living, including a supermarket, hardware shop, newsagents, hairdressing salon, off-licence, chemist, florist and a sub-post office. Lyefield Court also has a great advantage for golfers, as it adjoins Reading Golf Club!

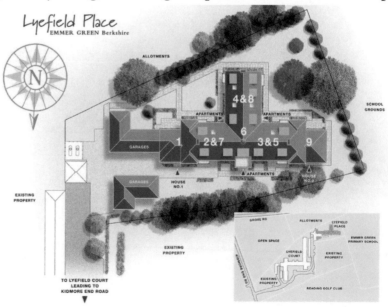

All other facilities - including a 30 - minute direct train service to central London - are available in Reading town centre, approximately two miles away.

Lyefield Court ~ Phase II

Apartments and Entrance

Wing house and Terrace

Chapter XIX

Closing One Chapter, Opening Another

Towards the end of 1999 I was suffering from serious breathing problems. I had developed a chest infection and, following a visit to a chest consultant, was diagnosed with chronic emphysema. It was entirely my own fault – I had been a very heavy smoker for many years – but although I had given up smoking in 1980 the damage had been done.

I needed to know the seriousness of my condition. My consultant warned me that I probably had less than three years to live.

The first consideration was to ensure the future of the English Courtyard Association. Chasophie Ltd., the Bonas Group's investment company, had financed all the English Courtyard Association's developments since its formation, through its construction company Geometer Developments. The relationship between the directors of the financing, development and management arms had always been close, as close as any can be between banker and client. All of us were colleagues, partners and friends. All of us related to the 'concept', and our partnership had existed for over 25 years. Benjamin Bonas' mother had bought a property at Manor Court, though sadly illness cut her tenure short. George Steer's mother had been one of my most enthusiastic supporters from the earliest days, whilst Christopher Thornhill's aunt had lived at Berrow Court, our second development, for nearly 15 years.

Since the prospect of my being around for any length of time appeared to be slim it seemed that the best way to protect, safeguard and guarantee the Association's future in the long term was by entering into a permanent partnership with Chasophie Ltd. and the Bonas Group, by allowing Geometer Developments to assume the name English Courtyard Developments. This would establish a strongly financed development and management organization under one common brand – English Courtyard – something which Christopher had wanted to do for some time but which, hitherto, I had always opposed.

Reassured that the future of English Courtyard was secure, in 2001 I moved into ECA's development at St. Luke's Court, Marlborough: the purchase of No 13 being jointly financed by Chasophie Ltd. and myself. Thus Chasophie generously honoured a promise, originally made to benefit my mother, by contributing instead to the purchase of a property at St. Luke's Court for me.

I enjoyed the experience enormously. I was able to see and appreciate at first hand the advantages of living at one of my own developments. The service of the Courtyard Managers, as well as the spaciousness and design of the house, met all the requirements one could need for a contented and stress-free retirement, the life I had originally expected my mother to enjoy at Manor Court, Pewsey, had she lived.

I spent an extremely happy year at St. Luke's Court. The decision to leave was not taken lightly. Fortunately, although still very breathless, my health had not deteriorated as expected; indeed my condition, if not improved, had at least stabilized. I remained Chairman of ECA and continued to devote my time to overseeing ECA's existing developments as well as being heavily involved in all new ones. I was also Chairman of the Elderly Accommodation Counsel, a charity dedicated to providing detailed information and advice for the elderly on the many different types of accommodation available to them throughout the UK, from the most expensive to the most economical, for those requiring independent living and those requiring specialised nursing care. It has an advisory service and a database second to none; it also hosts its own very successful Art Awards annually.

I am supplying full information about the Elderly Accommodation Counsel, a national charity, as it and its advice line could well prove extremely useful to anyone needing help or advice.

EAC may be contacted at their offices at: 89 Albert Embankment, London, SE1 7TP. Telephone: 0800 377 7070.

Email: enquiries@eac.org.uk   Website: www.eac.org.uk

Apart from the cost of running two homes (I had retained my cottage in the Savernake Forest, a mere two miles from St. Luke's Court), it seemed to me that having the still-active Chairman of the Association living at St. Luke's Court was rather an imposition on my fellow residents. I therefore let 13 St. Luke's Court for a year (the minimum period that ECA will allow a property to be let; rental can be very valuable for potential purchasers who want to know whether they like life on an ECA development before committing themselves), and returned to live in Savernake Forest. At the end of the year, I sold 13 St. Luke's Court to my tenants.

*****

Every good idea has its time. In the mid-1970s and 1980s, the English Courtyard Association revolutionized the retirement industry for the professional classes, setting standards of excellence in construction and management that were unequalled at that time, as the many prestigious awards it received from the National House Building Council, the Royal Institute of British Architects, the Department of the Environment and the Civic Trust clearly testify. Both Christopher and I had every reason to be proud of the heritage we had left behind. But ideas on their own are not enough when circumstances dictate otherwise.

From early January 2005 onwards – like the best laid plans of mice and men – the plans Christopher and I had so carefully laid for the English Courtyard Association started to fall apart dramatically, jeopardising its whole future.

Firstly the Bonas Group decided to sell English Courtyard Developments, and secondly Christopher Thornhill had a serious stroke. A temporary managing director was appointed by the Bonas Group to take over from Christopher, who was charged with putting the company into a sound financial position prior to a sale. This was completed in late 2006.

The purchaser, a young ambitious Irish property developer, completed the developments at Bearsted, Beaconsfield, Minchinhampton and Elton. But within a year, it was already clear that the 'new' ECD planned to turn itself into a much larger commercial empire and that the retirement sector was no longer its primary aim. The ethos and objectives of the two organizations – ECA and ECD – had become diametrically opposed to each other. There was no longer a common meeting point. It was in the best interests of both to part.

It was also becoming quite apparent that the development company had wildly over-extended itself financially at a time when the property market was already in recession.

In July 2007 I notified the development company that ECA intended to sever its connection with them, and wished to do so in an amicable way. But before the month was out ECD had gone into administration from which it never recovered, and it was left to me and the Board of the English Courtyard Association to pick up the pieces and provide for the future.

To ensure maximum resident involvement in the decisions that the Board had taken, and still needed to take, at my request, we appointed two additional Resident Directors. Sir Idris Pearce joined the Board in March 2007 and Angela Barker in August. We also appointed Christopher Mackenzie-Beevor as Operations Director, as back-up for our managing director Charles Clayton.

The fallout from the demise of the development company meant that three things required immediate action: to resurrect the Resales service (which since 2001 had been the responsibility of the development company); to provide ECA with a new website, the original ECD/ECA website having been withdrawn by ECD's creditors; and to pay Courtyard Managers their Resales commissions, which they had not received from the development company due to it going into administration.

It was of the utmost importance that neither ECA's loyal staff nor those residents depending upon English Courtyard's Resales service should suffer as a result of ECD going into administration. All the above were addressed, and Christopher

Mackenzie-Beevor, almost single-handed, set up the new ECA website from scratch and had it running within a few months – no mean achievement.

For some years Henry Thornton, joint founder of Beechcroft Developments and the Beechcroft Trust, had expressed an interest in joining forces with the English Courtyard Association. At the time neither Christopher Thornhill nor I had felt the wish or the need for this. However, a chance telephone call from Henry Thornton on 1 May 2007 made me think that the time had come to consider the advantages of a merger with the Beechcroft Trust. With English Courtyard Developments in administration, it seemed the right time to explore the possibility seriously. There were obviously potential advantages to both organizations.

Beechcroft Trust's situation needs explanation. In 2002 Henry Thornton and his partner Guy Mossop sold Beechcroft Developments to John Laing, an old established family building firm. But, very shortly afterwards, Laing's property development division was sold to George Wimpey (today Taylor Wimpey). As Wimpey were not interested in the retirement field, the opportunity arose for a management buy-out of Beechcroft Developments. This resulted in Beechcroft Developments being acquired by their managing director Chris Thompson. However, Henry Thornton and Guy Mossop retained control of the management company – The Beechcroft Trust – and the management of their original 22 developments. This resulted in there being two Beechcroft companies – Beechcroft Developments and The Beechcroft Trust – two totally different companies and now quite unconnected, but both trading under the name 'Beechcroft'.

Furthermore, the Trust's management was stretched, and its core needed strengthening. Therefore, a merger with the English Courtyard Association allowed it to operate under a different name, strengthen its management and become part of a national organization. Whereas the Beechcroft Trust's 22 developments operated largely in the Home Counties, the English Courtyard Association's 38 developments covered 21 counties and Guernsey.

From an ECA perspective the merger allowed us to strengthen our senior management, which was becoming fragile, not least due to the health and age of several of our Board members. Only Charles Clayton and Christopher Mackenzie-Beevor were below official retirement age, and ECA needed new blood – new blood that had stature, and that understood the importance of ECA's ethos and would ensure that it would be maintained. Beechcroft Trust's directors brought with them skills in business, banking, sales and marketing, skills mostly supplied previously by Christopher Thornhill, Stephen Alexander and myself.

However, to me, far and away the most important skill ECA required from the merger was Henry Thornton's own development skills. Under his leadership Beechcroft Developments, before its sale, had built 22 first-class retirement developments, any of which ECA would have been proud to claim as our own. Henry Thornton appeared to me to be the ideal replacement for Christopher Thornhill. With Henry overseeing the construction of new and exciting developments, combined with Charles Clayton's management skills (resulting from twenty years of successfully managing ECA as Regional Manager, General Manager and Managing Director), the new organization should be in good hands as long as it respected the importance of the ECA and BT brands, and maintained and used the achievements of the past when building for the future.

The name for the new company, providing the merger was approved by ECA and BT's residents and Boards, was to be Cognatum Ltd.(*Cognatum*, in Latin, means 'bringing together'): the bringing together of the English Courtyard Association and the Beechcroft Trust.

Before any final decision was made, I spent a month visiting every single one of our developments (except Guernsey) and holding meetings with residents at all ECA's 38 developments. I listened to residents' concerns and reassured them that the merger was in their best interests. In particular, I made it clear that the name English Courtyard Association would remain and would appear on all advertising. The Courtyard Manager Service and the Courtyard Managers' duties, which residents had previously enjoyed and about which they and the Courtyard Managers were most concerned, would remain exactly the same. As the services offered by BT and ECA were different, BT owners would continue to receive the BT service and ECA residents the ECA service. I was also able to announce that all Courtyards would have computers and all Courtyard Managers would be expected to be computer literate.

The two organizations would move to new offices and through economies of scale – merging the accounts staff, etc – substantial savings could be made to the service charge. A new Resales organization – Cognatum Property Ltd – would be set up that would be affiliated to Cognatum, and John Lowe would join the new company as its Sales Director. It was intended that 50% of all profits from the Resales service would be returned to Cognatum Ltd. It was expected, in time, that Cognatum Property Ltd would be able to contribute a useful addition to residents' reserve funds. I also made it clear that, once the property market improved, Cognatum would undertake new developments in partnership with suitable private developers. This would be arranged and controlled by Henry Thornton. It was underlined that there would be no financial risk to Cognatum.

By the spring of 2010, Cognatum's headquarters had been established at Glebe Barn, Cuxham, Near Watlington, Oxfordshire. I was to be the new Life President, Henry Thornton the Chairman, and Charles Clayton the Managing Director. A new chapter had opened.

Chapter XX

Epilogue and Unfinished Business

The English Courtyard Association was never about achieving personal wealth. In the pre- and post-war period I was privileged to have a happy carefree childhood spent in beautiful English countryside, living in the faded elegance of three glorious rambling village rectories in North Yorkshire. Regrettably, serious scholastic achievement was sacrificed to a preference for the cricket field; I adopted the all-too-familiar schoolboy policy that all that was necessary was to just 'scrape through'! A fascinating and enjoyable period of commissioned service in the Scots Guards followed: in Germany, during the years of occupation; in Canada and America in the 1950s-60s; in Kenya for two wonderful years, prior to its Independence in November 1963, when I first met Phyllis. These were interspersed with London Duties and the amazing spoiling London social scene of the late 50s and early 60s, all shared with a wide circle of like-minded lifetime friends, who – in fairness to them – probably took a more serious attitude to life and at an earlier age than did I! One of the things that still gives me the greatest pleasure is that a large number of the friends with whom I served had family members who later came to live at one or other of ECA's 37 developments. Indeed, one even had a mother living at one ECA development whilst his father lived at another – certainly loyalty above average!

The previous 40 years may have been about having a good time, but the next 40 years – after my major car accident in August 1971 – were 'payback time': payback time for the huge sacrifices made by my parents and their generation in order to give me – and others of my generation – a magnificent start in life, in terms of values, education and opportunity. One thing remained a constant, that of a wonderful and happy life. I always used to say, to anyone that suggested otherwise, that I had never done a day's work in my life! That is absolutely true, and remains so. How can you have done any work if all you are doing is having a good time, and spending it with those whose company you enjoy and whose ability you respect?

How enormously fortunate I have been, and how incredibly lucky. I always used to tease Phyllis that there was someone 'up there' looking after her, so frequently were near mishaps, or potential serious disasters averted. Although that was undoubtedly true, it is probably even truer that the same person has looked – and indeed is still looking – after me!

It is not work, it is a thing of wonder and joy to see an idea come to fruition First finding a suitable site, then designing detailed plans for the purpose, seeing the buildings and grounds gradually evolve from empty shells into things of beauty, meeting those interested in living them, learning from them and about them, and finally seeing them turn your plans into their home – each with its own characteristics, individual identity and feel – all this is only exceeded by, as the years pass, seeing that the home and the lifestyle it offered them has indeed worked and fulfilled their needs.

Perhaps 2012 is a good time to consider what things we could have done differently, what we might have changed, and what remains undone.

The stated aim of ECA was to provide spacious accommodation in a traditional English setting, offering security and support through our Courtyard Manager Service, for like-minded people from the professions, business, rural and similar backgrounds, who wished to be able to maintain an independent life with dignity, 'from early retirement onwards'.

1. An ageing population

On the whole, the aim has been achieved and the quality of life maintained, but one thing which we should have recognized in our desire to provide independent living, and perhaps done more to address, was the change in residents' needs over time. The average age at Manor Court in 1980 was 64 and at least three-quarters of the residents were married. They regularly entertained in their own homes, enjoyed a good social life with family, friends and other residents, and travelled extensively. But time brought about enforced changes of circumstance. Couples lost husband or wife: their ability to entertain and socialise became more difficult, and in many cases loneliness and ill health became a factor. A few years ago the average age at Manor Court reached 89.

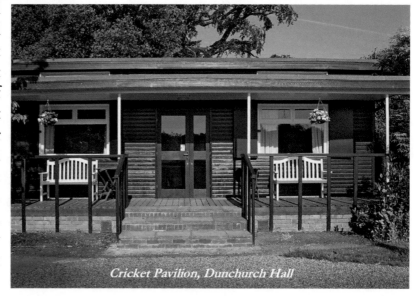
Cricket Pavilion, Dunchurch Hall

There are two ECA developments, in particular, where it has been possible to alleviate the problems of ageing and loneliness, because of the facilities that they possess. These are at Church Place, Ickenham, which has a magnificently renovated Barn, used by residents for communal and private functions, and at Dunchurch Hall, Dunchurch, where there is a splendidly renovated cricket pavilion.

The latter is ideal: large enough to have meetings and social gatherings, art classes, computer instruction classes, and flower arrangement, gardening and local history classes, as well as classes in all manner of subjects in conjunction with the local branch of the University of the Third Age. Residents can have picnics on the grass with grand-children without causing a nuisance to others. This is relatively easy to replicate, at an affordable cost, on many of ECA's developments. At both Ickenham and Dunchurch events are suggested by the residents and a residents' committee co-ordinates the use that their recreational accommodation offers, together with input from their Courtyard Managers. I am reliably informed by those that live there that loneliness is not a concern.

If ECA was starting today, I would ensure that a Dunchurch-style pavilion/summer house, together with tea and coffee-making facilities, existed at all our developments. The cost of installation would not be great and it should be possible to do it, even today. Most ECA sites have the land and space to accommodate one, and I know several Courtyards are keen to do so. I believe their wish should be supported

2. Affordability

One of the few disappointments arising from ECA's success is the steady — sometimes swift — increase in the price of our properties, at new developments in particular, caused by inflation and market conditions. This has led to a number of potential purchasers, who either visited or read about our developments — and needed and wanted the lifestyle we had to offer — finding that they could no longer afford them.

For many years this has been a concern I have wished to address: an interest that coincided with my interest in equity release — a residents' option to liquidate their property assets into cash or additional income, something requested by many ECA residents over the years.

Indeed, together with my good friend and former banker Gay Gardner, I even became involved in the formation of a company, Retirement Plus — initially in conjunction with the property giant British Land — in order to provide this.

Since 2008 market conditions have changed and taken their toll, but even in 2012 equity release is still available from a number of sources and in a number of forms, although independent professional financial advice should always be sought before taking any decision to use it. It is interesting to note that its use is being advocated, where appropriate, in recent reports on retirement issued by both Hanover Housing Association and leading estate agents Knight Frank.

However, my principle interest — harking back to chapter VII on Home for Life — remains the need for a Life Lease or Lifetime-Let using an Equity Release/Reverse Mortgage scheme to make the purchase of ECA property more affordable. This scheme would enable those wishing to invest only the minimum sum in the purchase of an ECA property, in order to downsize and/or provide themselves with a secure home in their retirement, to do so. For example – as shown below – it would enable a couple aged 75 a 44% reduction on the full price to acquire a Life Lease or Lifetime-Let, and more if they are older or single. This scheme would apply to anyone wishing to purchase any freehold or long leasehold property which they deemed suitable for their retirement. It would also enable more children to purchase a Life Lease or Lifetime-Let for an elderly parent or parents.

A Life Lease or Lifetime-Let requires the purchase to be made jointly by the occupiers – or their family or friends – with a bank, finance company or large property company. The property, or the balance of the lease, would be purchased and owned jointly by the occupier and the finance house. The amount each would pay would be dependent on the age and life expectancy of the occupier, who would receive the same security of tenure as a freeholder – and without the fear of unknown future rent increases – since by purchasing a Life Lease or Lifetime Let the purchaser would have paid in full, in advance. The right scheme would almost certainly ensure the refund of a proportion of the initial price, should the death of one or both occupants occur much earlier than would have been expected. Conversely, should the occupant or occupants live longer than expected, their right to live there would be safeguarded, as the Lease or Let would be for life.

The figures below are for example only. They were provided in 2008 by a market leader, and will certainly have changed. Risk will have changed, as will life expectancy figures, but the principle remains the same.

Life Lease/Lifetime Let	Property Value			
	£200,000	£300,000	£400,000	£500,000
Single male age 75 cost	£100,800	£157,200	£209,600	£262,000
Single male age 80 cost	£90,680	£142,020	£189,360	£236,700
Single female age 75 cost	£117,800	£182,700	£243,600	£304,500
Single female age 80 cost	£96,240	£150,360	£200,480	£250,600
M&F both age 75 cost	£111,120	£172,680	£230,240	£287,280
M&F both age 80 cost	£104,120	£162,180	£216,240	£270,300

Such a scheme could be invaluable for elderly retired people of limited means, who are in need of affordable security in their advancing years, as well as for their children. The potential benefits are extensive: they could even assist parents to buy a Life Lease or a Lifetime-Let in their own home, thus enabling them to hand over the family home to their children during the last 10 or so years of their lives, to minimise their inheritance liability whilst continuing to be able to live there.

Certainly it is a cause worth fighting for, even though it may have to wait until financial markets recover their stability. I hope too that readers who recognize its significance and potential – and who are able to influence such matters, particularly bankers, financiers, property companies, politicians and members of the press – will also investigate this need and fight and argue its case. Such a scheme, with proper financial resources, requires little more than good actuarial calculations on life expectancy in order to make it viable and successful for both the provider and those for whom it is provided. It just needs the drive, the imagination and the will to make it happen. But it must be fair to both parties.

3. Grace and Favour Charity

A third important innovation I would like to see is the formation of a charity, a subsidiary of the English Courtyard Association. The Association owns the freeholds of probably the finest retirement properties in existence. Its management is entirely non-profit making. With 37 developments of its own, 74 resales are likely to be generated and come on the market each year, on average two per development per year. The leases of ECA's properties can be owned by companies, institutions, charities or private donors, or left to the charity in wills – perhaps by former ECA residents or their families. The purpose of the charity would be to allow leases of ECA's resale properties to be bought by any of the above, and donated to the charity. Any gifted property would then become the equivalent of a 'grace and favour' property, and those donating a property would, as donors, retain the nomination rights for that property. A dream? I don't believe so. The whole ECA story was a dream, and it happened. Once this book is complete perhaps I will be able to help organize it.

4. Solar energy

This subject has been raised at a number of the Residents' Meetings which I have chaired in recent years. From what my architects tell me, having looked into the possibility, the cost of installing it in ECA's existing developments would be too expensive to be of benefit to our residents, so they would not recommend it. This is apart from any undesirable architectural effect its installation could have on the classical design of our buildings, which could make it unacceptable. Many of our buildings are in conservation areas, or are listed. Nonetheless, the possibility should be reviewed periodically as new technology advances, improves and becomes more cost-effective. However, there is no doubt that the use of solar energy should be explored and considered in any new developments at the design stage, and incorporated as and if appropriate.

5. In support of the English Apple

This next thought is not my own – and it is easily achievable. It is also very English, and therefore appropriate for an English Courtyard Association development! A good friend of mine, Philippa Davenport, who for 35 years was the food correspondent of the Financial Times, has in recent months been fighting the cause of the English apple! In my childhood our orchards were filled with many local varieties of the English apple. Today our shops are filled with apples that either are not English or are grown because they are the most commercial, like Bramleys or Cox's. If we are not careful many of the old English brands will become extinct. That would be sad. ECA developments cover 21 counties, as well as Guernsey. We have space for English apple trees, not least because apple trees need not take up a great amount of space. You can have dwarf apple trees, or shape them like a fan against a wall. The Association could house two or three local varieties on each development, and we would be looking after our heritage!

6. Keeping in touch with our residents

The success of the Association has not only been its buildings, its grounds and its Courtyard Manager Service, it has also been the close relationship maintained by its founders and senior management with ECA residents. This is extremely important. For many years I made a point of knowing every resident personally. It was a privilege and a delight to do so. I was reminded of its importance by residents only recently when on a visit to the Midlands. Surveys, excellent control of budgets and expenditure are no substitute for personal hands-on contact with residents.

Obviously as the organization increases in size this becomes more difficult, but it should be possible for Regional Managers to ensure that they know every resident in their region personally. This would mean not waiting until residents have a problem but being proactive, asking to meet them in order to get to know them. We have so much to learn from our residents and by listening to them: their fascinating lives, and their requirements and needs in a changing world. They have so much to teach us about changing with the times!

7. Spreading the Word

A final word: we need to let people – potential purchasers and their children – know just how much life at an English Courtyard Association development has to offer so many people from early retirement onwards. We can do this through the national and local press, through national, local and trade magazines, through charities and the providers of services for the retired, and by holding Open Weekends and opening our grounds, at each development, once a year in conjunction with a major national or local charity, by studying and learning from the means of communication practised by our children and grand-children.

'I don't want to live there – it's an old persons' home!' is a typical comment frequently heard from those who have no idea of the quality of life that is available to them. They ignore too the great contributions they could make to the lives of other like-minded residents, which in turn could make their own lives more worthwhile as well as perhaps more enjoyable. We need to be clear: the vast majority of people who might aspire to what the Association has to offer have never heard of us. It is our duty to put that right. This is the conversation we need to have, not only with the press and service providers but with our residents, with their children, and throughout the Association. There are many ways of going about it. This book is just one step along the road.

SO, PLEASE LET'S SHARE OUR SECRET.

Dunchurch Hall

Chapter XXI

The Architects' Story
by Richard Morton

Left to Right: Richard Morton, Giles Downes, Paul Gibson

The architectural sub-plot to the story of the English Courtyard Association is fascinating in its own right because in the mid-1970s, when the ECA concept was emerging, the great majority of architects did not consider 'traditional' design suitable for new buildings.

From a late start in the UK with Lubetkin's Highpoint flats in Highgate in the 1930s, 'modern architecture' had by the 1960s come to be seen as the only intellectually respectable type of design. A comparison between the cathedrals in Liverpool is interesting, separated as they are by only about 50 years. Giles Gilbert Scott's Anglican cathedral is to all intents and purposes a fully-fledged gothic design but by the time its Catholic neighbour was designed in the 1960s only a 'modern' solution could be considered. In London, meanwhile, the destruction of Philip Hardwick's Greek classical arch at Euston and the near-demolition of the St Pancras Hotel demonstrated the complete disregard for the styles of the nineteenth century.

Housing development at the time was dominated by the same thinking. Pitched roofs were out of the question for any architect who wanted to be taken seriously and Adolf Loos' dictum that 'ornament is crime' was still taken as gospel.

170

Paul Gibson, when he took up Noel Shuttleworth's commission, was fully versed in this modernist gospel having worked first for Norman Foster and then for Farrell Grimshaw on some of the earliest 'high-tech' buildings at the cutting edge of modernism. He soon began, however, to show signs of a very different type of architectural thinking. To most of his generation traditional design was seen as morally wrong and intellectually flawed, but Paul began to move to a different view – that there could be little wrong with designs which respected their surroundings in terms of form, character, scale, materials and detailing. In his earliest designs at Pewsey, Wadhurst, Upton, Lenham and Emmer Green, Paul took what was then the brave step for an architect of studying the site and its surroundings and using local materials in traditional ways to create quietly beautiful buildings.

Helping Paul almost from the outset was Giles Downes who had come from the same modernist background as Paul. Together they worked to deliver schemes which were distinctive, not only in their welcoming of tradition, but in the quality of their detailing and in their emphasis on the creation of fine buildings set in beautiful landscaped spaces.

Gradually this discreetly revolutionary approach gained recognition in terms of critical coverage (an article by Gillian Darley in the Architectural Review was noteworthy) and of awards. In 1983 the schemes at Pewsey, Wadhurst and Upton all received RIBA/DoE Housing Design Awards – three of only nine awards given that year – and this exceptional feat was repeated in 1987 with the awards this time going to the developments at Lenham, Emmer Green and Puddletown. In 1989 the quality of the work was recognised by Prince Charles in his book A Vision of Britain.

A notable feature of the early schemes, and one which was to continue through the entire English Courtyard oeuvre, was the emphasis on the use of the best local details and materials: handmade Swallow tiles at Crittles Court, Ham Hill stone at South Petherton and Ilminster, Chilmark stone and beautifully knapped flint at Earls Manor Court. Over in Guernsey for the work at Les Blancs Bois, a nearby quarry was specially reopened to supply the traditional rubble granite; when there were some teething problems after the gales of 1990, with damp coming through, the locals said, 'Didn't they tell you Guernsey granite always does that?'

In the late 1980s, with the English Courtyard work gathering pace, Sidell Gibson won a competition for Grand Buildings, a large scheme in Trafalgar Square, and this was to lead to a huge expansion in the firm's work, taking them to their current place as one of the country's largest practices. To help carry forward English Courtyard's work in the middle of this expansion Richard Morton joined the team working with Paul and Giles, and the three of them worked as a team for the next 15 years.

Paul retired in 2001 to pursue his other love, painting, and now divides his time between Wiltshire and Malta.

Giles took his deep knowledge of traditional construction and materials, developed while working on English Courtyard schemes, to new heights when we won the competition for the redesign of much of Windsor Castle after the fire. He recently retired as a partner, but continues to work at Sidell Gibson, has a deep involvement with the Carpenters' Company and other craft organisations, and also works as a sculptor.

Richard remains as a partner at Sidell Gibson, working with many of the country's leading specialists in housing for older people – Beechcroft, Anchor, Hanover and Barchester among others – and it is through that work that The English Courtyard Association's architectural soul goes marching on.

Chapter XXII

ECA's Housing Design Awards

DoE, NHBC and RIBA Housing Design Awards
1983   Manor Court, Pewsey
1983   Crittles Court, Wadhurst
1983   Berrow Court - Highly Commended
1987   Walpole Court, Puddletown
1987   Atwater Court, Lenham
1987   Lyefield Court, Emmer Green
1989   The Vinery, Torquay
1991   Malthouse Court, Towcester
1993   Earls Manor Court, Winterbourne Earls
1993   Framers Court, Lane End

Civic Trust Awards
1982   Berrow Court – Commendation
1986   Lyefield Court - Commendation
1988   Walpole Court - Commendation
1990   Les Blancs Bois, Guernsey - Commendation
1995   Earls Manor Court – Commendation
1995   Framers Court – Commendation
1999   Bluecoat Pond, Christ's Hospital - Mention

Stone Federation Design Awards for Natural Stone
1989   Les Blancs Bois, Guernsey - Highly Commended
1991   Ashcombe Court, Ilminster - Commendation

The Daily Telegraph What House Awards - 16 in total including:
2001   Fordingbridge - Best Retirement Development
2002   Fordingbridge - Best Landscape Design
2003   Prestbury - Best Retirement Development
2005   Bournemouth - Best Landscape

Local Design Awards - 11 in total

Britannia National Homebuilder Design Awards
2002   St Luke's Court, Wiltshire - Best Restoration & Conversion - Commendation
2002   St Luke's Court, Wiltshire - Best Landscaping of a Development – Commendation
2003   Timbermill Court, Fordingbridge - Best Landscape

Landscape Design Awards - 30 in total

Evening Standard Awards - 5 in total including:
2004   Muskerry Court, Tunbridge Wells - Silver in Best Small Development

Daily Mail UK Property Awards
2007   Stuart Court, Minchinhampton - Best Retirement Development

Mail on Sunday British Homes Awards
2008   Stuart Court, Minchinhampton - Best Retirement

Index

Printed in Great Britain
by Amazon.co.uk, Ltd.,
Marston Gate.